STRATEGY

—— *for* ——

YOU

Building *a* Bridge *to* the Life You Want

RICH HORWATH

GREENLEAF
BOOK GROUP PRESS

Published by Greenleaf Book Group Press
Austin, Texas
www.gbgpress.com

Copyright ©2012 Rich Horwath

Distributed by Greenleaf Book Group LLC

For ordering information or special discounts for bulk purchases, please contact Greenleaf Book Group LLC at PO Box 91869, Austin, TX 78709, 512.891.6100.

Design and composition by Greenleaf Book Group LLC and Bumpy Design
Cover design by Greenleaf Book Group LLC
Bridge illustrations on inside pages by Ron Magnes

Publisher's Cataloging-In-Publication Data
(Prepared by The Donohue Group, Inc.)
Horwath, Rich.
   Strategy for you : building a bridge to the life you want / Rich Horwath. — 1st ed.
    p. : ill. ; cm.
    ISBN: 978-1-60832-251-0
   1. Self-realization. 2. Conduct of life. 3. Personal coaching. I. Title.
BF637.S4 H67 2012
158.1   2011932970

Part of the Tree Neutral® program, which offsets the number of trees consumed in the production and printing of this book by taking proactive steps, such as planting trees in direct proportion to the number of trees used: www.treeneutral.com

Printed in the United States of America on acid-free paper

11 12 13 14 15 16   10 9 8 7 6 5 4 3 2 1

First Edition

CONTENTS

For Mom and Pop,
inspiration and foundation of my bridge.

ACKNOWLEDGMENTS

Thanks to my wife, Anne, for her love, positive spirit, and commitment to nurturing a wonderful family. Thanks to our children, Luke and Jessica, for filling our home with love and laughter. I am eternally grateful to my parents, Jan and Rich, and sister, Sharon, for the blessings that come from growing up in a healthy, happy family.

I'd like to thank the following business leaders for providing me with their wisdom and insights through our work together: Chris Anderson, Craig Besler, Jerry Casey, Andrew de Guttadauro, Steve Denault, Domenick DiCindio, Tom Fordonski, Valerie Gerbino, Dean Gregory, Jeff Haas, David Hammond, Robert Hanf, Paul Hardy, Matt Hodson, Todd Hunt, Jim Immormino, Ranndy Kellogg, Oliver Konarkowski, Rick Kosturko, Steve Lamb, Richard Locke, Michael Mehler, Brian Meinken, Pete Menary, Bill Mosteller, Tim O'Connor, Bob Palumbo, Joe Palumbo, Don Pogorzelski, Sharon Ryan, Jeffrey Sanfilippo, Jasper Sanfilippo Jr., Janet Schijns, Rob Schneider, Bob Schruender, Regina Shanklin, Dale Snyder, Rich Stewart, Mark Sutter, Joe Talanges, Norman Tashash, Dave Taylor, Phil Tegeler, Mike Valentine, Chris Varcoe, Terry Walsh, and John Zgombic.

Finally a special thanks to the amazing team at Greenleaf Book Group for their wonderful work throughout the publishing process: Tanya Hall, Chris McRay, Bill Crawford, Neil Gonzalez, Lari Bishop, Kristen Sears, Kris Pauls, Theresa Reding, Jenn McMurray, and the entire group.

INTRODUCTION

THE GREATEST DAY
OF YOUR LIFE

*Recall yesterday,
think today,
envision tomorrow.*

One Saturday morning a couple of years ago, my five-year-old son, Luke, bounded down the stairs for breakfast, shouting, "Dad, are you ready for the greatest day of your life?"

Stunned by the enormity of the question, I enthusiastically replied, "Yes!" and he proceeded to outline exactly what that day would look like: making chocolate chip pancakes for breakfast, creating a new Thomas the Train track layout, hitting golf balls in the backyard, grilling cheese sandwiches for lunch, playing trucks in the sandbox, swinging on the swing set, watching *Cars*, grilling hot dogs for dinner, and to cap it all off, toasting marshmallows on the bonfire. Indeed, it would arguably be the greatest day of his young life.

We made our way through that beautiful spring day, cleaning pancake batter off the cabinets, searching for golf balls in the woods, burning the first of the grilled cheese sandwiches, and swinging higher and higher into the cloudless blue sky. Later that night, as we told ghost stories around the crackling bonfire, licking gooey marshmallows off our fingertips, Luke said, "We did it."

"Did what?" I asked.

"Had the greatest day of our lives," he replied.

And we had.

Whether it's in your work or your personal life, the opportunity to envision and create your greatest days is within your reach. You can begin the journey by asking yourself two questions:

What would be the greatest day of my life?

How would I get there?

Strategy as a Bridge

Hiking through the woods, you come across a stream. It's only a few feet deep and fewer than ten feet across. With several hours of hiking ahead, you'd like to continue on with dry feet. Fifty yards to the right, you notice a log resting across the stream, several feet above the water. You walk over and place your right foot on the log to test its steadiness. It appears sound, so you step onto the log with both feet and carefully walk across. Hopping off, you look back with a feeling of accomplishment before hiking on.

While it wasn't a death-defying act—after all, you didn't daringly cross a shaky structure hundreds of feet above roaring white rapids—you did manage to get from where you were to where you wanted to go. And for thousands of years, bridges have helped people do just that. Natural or man-made, a bridge is a structure that spans and provides passage over a gap or barrier, such as a river or roadway. A bridge can be simple, like a basic wooden beam, or it can be complex, like a double-decked bridge. It can be short (e.g., a small covered bridge) or long (such as the record-setting Akashi Kaikyo Bridge in Japan, spanning 12,828 feet). It can be old and unstable, or it can be a breathtaking work of art.

In its simplest form, strategy is a bridge for getting from where you are today to where you want to go. Whether in business or in your personal life, strategy is how you plan to get from your current position to your desired goals. A bridge provides passage over a gap—something that's missing. For many of us, there are gaps in our lives—things that are missing, things that we'd like to have more of, such as more time with family and friends, more purposeful work, a healthier lifestyle, and greater spirituality. Strategy can help us fill those gaps.

A bridge also spans barriers. Think about the barriers you face, the obstacles and adversity—a difficult coworker, making your financial numbers at work, weakening relationships with your kids, high cholesterol, and so forth. Strategy can help us span and overcome these obstacles.

Depending on their design, most bridges have the following forces distributed throughout their structure: compression (pushing force), tension (pulling force), torsion (twisting of an object), and bending (turning in a particular direction). A poorly designed bridge crumbles under these forces. A well-designed bridge intelligently blends these forces with one another to actually increase its strength and stability.

Like a bridge, a sound strategy for living blends these forces to enable us to withstand adversity and overcome challenges. Without a sound strategy for our lives, we allow all kinds of forces to push, pull, twist, and turn us into mental and emotional pretzels. Our inability to say "no" *pushes* us into time-wasting activities; a lack of strategic direction allows us to be *pulled* down a career path we never wanted; good intentions to volunteer in the community are *twisted* into negative comments when we're not able to meet the time commitments; and we're emotionally *turned* around when the relationship we let wither finally ends. With a solid strategy in place, however, we can harness the everyday forces to lead us where we want to go.

Without a strategy, we have no clear way to get to where we want to go. Without a strategy, we risk falling into the gaps and being held back by the barriers. Without a strategy, we are powerless to create the life we want. But *with* a strategy, there are no limits to how far our bridge can take us. We can build a bridge to the greatest days of our lives.

The Bridge to Nowhere

Think about where you are today. Do you enjoy your job? Is your mind active and fully engaged? Are you physically healthy? Are your finances solid? Are your relationships inspiring and supportive? Now think about the bridge that led you to your current position. Was it planned and well thought-out, or was it more similar to Alaska's infamous Gravina Island Bridge, often referred to as the $398 million "bridge to nowhere"?

The most common example I run into involves career satisfaction. When I ask people to trace the bridge of events leading up to their current job, it tends to go like this:

> When I was finishing college, my dad had a friend who was the VP of sales for a paper company. Since I wasn't getting any real job opportunities from the on-campus recruiting, I interviewed with the paper company and took a job in sales. I worked there for three years and then received a call from a headhunter for a position with another paper company for $10,000 more in salary. I moved over to that company in sales but was asked to take a position in customer service six months later when they eliminated a bunch of sales territories. Two years later, a friend of mine said her company was hiring for a position in IT that interfaced with customers and marketing. I interviewed and got the job, but I wound up doing mostly data entry for the marketing team. I'm nearly ten years into my career now and doing IT work I can't stand.

This story of an individual's bridge to nowhere would be amusing if it weren't so true. Think about it: The average working adult spends about fifty hours a week working and commuting to work. Multiply those fifty hours by fifty weeks, and you have 2,500 hours a year that are potentially being wasted in a role that's either not fulfilling, not enjoyable, or both. Over the course of a career, that's more than 100,000 hours!

We all have resources to varying degrees, consisting of time, talent, and money. How we use those resources each day determines our level of happiness and success in four areas: Mind, Body, Relationships, and Finances. Are you investing your time in activities that keep your mind actively engaged? Are you investing your talent in work that is valued? Are you investing yourself in relationships that strengthen the bonds of family, friends, and colleagues? Are you investing finances to ensure longer-term prosperity?

A Gallup survey confirmed just how widespread the lack of individual strategy has become. Canvassing its database of 1.7 million employees, Gallup found that only 20 percent feel their jobs match up with their strengths.[1] That is, only two out of ten people believe they have an opportunity each day to do what they're best at. If we haven't planned to match our passions and strengths with our professional and personal lives, then we can only watch with regret as our days slip away like the grains of sand in an hourglass.

Strategy can save us.

In the world of business, strategy can make or break a company. Research by Paul Carroll and Chunka Mui, published in the *Harvard Business Review*, showed that the number one cause of bankruptcy is bad strategy.[2] Companies of all shapes and sizes have closed their doors because they didn't have a plan for success—particularly in economic downturns. If you don't have a strategic plan today, you may not have a business tomorrow.

The same holds true for individuals. *Sports Illustrated* reported that 60 percent of professional basketball players are in serious financial trouble within five years of retirement, despite earning millions of dollars a year while they held that job.[3] According to Yahoo! Sports, Scottie Pippen, named one of the top fifty NBA players of all time, lost his career earnings of $120 million in bad investments.[4] Still think having lots of money protects you from personal bankruptcy? The sobering fact remains, if you don't have a strategy, you may not have a future—at least, not the one you want.

A Plan (or Not) for Life

To determine how effectively people are planning for successful lives, I conducted research in partnership with Harris Interactive, involving 2,257 adults of all ages, from eighteen to fifty-five-plus years old, from across the United States. Participants' educational backgrounds varied, from incomplete high school to postgraduate college degrees, and incomes ranged from less than $35,000 per year to greater than $75,000 per year. The study found only 15 percent of adults have a written plan for their life that outlines their goals and the strategies for achieving them. Based on this representative sample, we can conclude that fewer than two out of every ten Americans have a plan for their life.

I conducted a second study, involving more than three hundred Fortune 1000 business executives, to see if the practice of developing a strategic plan for their business carried over to their personal lives. These leaders consisted of chief executives, presidents, executive directors, general managers, and vice presidents representing more than twenty-five industries across the United States. When asked the question "Do you have a written strategic plan for your business?" 82 percent of executives responded "yes." However, when faced with the question "Do you have a written strategic plan for your life?" only 22 percent responded "yes."

Data has shown that organizations without a sound strategy go bankrupt. In the long run, they fail. Despite the overwhelming evidence that a business needs a strong strategic plan to survive, by far the majority of people working in business haven't applied those same strategy principles for success to their personal lives. Why? No one has ever shown them how.

Strategy Defined

Do you remember the first time you fell in love? Can you describe the feeling? A quickening heart beat, flushing cheeks, butterflies in the stomach, a tingling throughout the body. All good descriptors. But can you *define* love? A concrete definition is more difficult. Why? Because love is an abstract concept. We can't reach out and touch it. It's intangible.

The same can be said for strategy. Just like love or leadership, strategy is an abstract, intangible concept. Defining it is difficult. However, if we're going to embark on a system for developing strategy for our lives, we'll need a common understanding of what it means:

Strategy is a plan for using your resources—time, talent, and money—to achieve your goals.

Strategy is how we get from where we are today to where we want to be in the future—to the achievement of our goals. As discussed earlier, strategy is a bridge, taking us from one point to the next, spanning gaps and helping us to pass over barriers. It can enable us to reach our full potential in terms of our mind, our body, our relationships, and our finances.

Let's break down the pieces of the definition even further.

"STRATEGY IS A PLAN . . ."

Strategy doesn't just happen. A plan requires thinking, and thinking requires us to invest time in considering what we want to achieve (our goal) and how to go about doing it (our strategy).

". . . FOR USING YOUR RESOURCES—TIME, TALENT, AND MONEY . . ."

From both a business and a personal perspective, we all have resources—time, talent, and money—to varying degrees. How effectively we use, or allocate, our resources determines how effective, successful, and happy we'll be.

". . . TO ACHIEVE YOUR GOALS."

A *goal* is what we're trying to achieve; it's the general target. Before we can ever set a strategy, we first need to understand exactly what it is we want to achieve. Just as you couldn't build a bridge without first determining where it must lead, you can't develop a strategy for your life without first understanding where it is you want to go.

The Five-Step Plan

My work as a business strategist is to help managers develop the strategies that will, in essence, create the bridge to their greatest business performance. During the past ten years working as a chief strategy officer and founder of the Strategic Thinking Institute, I developed tools and frameworks to help multimillion- and even multibillion-dollar organizations identify their business goals and the strategies for reaching them. I had never, however, helped people apply these business strategy principles for success in their individual lives—until now.

Strategy for You is intended to provide you with a five-step plan for creating a bridge to the life you want. It is unlike other books in that it takes the foundational principles of business strategy and helps you apply them to your life. The result is a simple plan you can follow to become effective, successful, and happy at work and at home.

The *Strategy for You* five-step plan includes the following elements:

STEP 1: DISCOVER—SELECTING YOUR BRIDGE'S LOCATION

Just as you can't build a bridge without first determining the starting and finishing points, you can't build a strategy for your life without understanding where you're starting from and where you want to go. The Discover step is the process of uncovering your purpose—what you want and why. Purpose takes the form of a mission, a vision, goals, and objectives.

STEP 2: DIFFERENTIATE—IMAGINING YOUR BRIDGE'S STYLE

Bridges come in all shapes and sizes, from small, wooden covered structures to shiny, sweeping waves of metal. Their differences begin in the mind of the designer. The Differentiate step requires you to identify the unique characteristics of your personal bridge. These elements include your individual combination of strengths, weaknesses, background, and abilities that set you apart from the pack. To *differentiate* means to deviate from the norm in ways that people value.

STEP 3: DECIDE—CHOOSING YOUR BRIDGE'S MATERIALS

Before a bridge can be built, the designer must decide which materials to use, based on functional needs, the size of the span to be crossed, and desired aesthetics. All these choices require trade-offs. The Decide step involves the process of allocating your resources—time, talent, and money—to achieve your goals. The act of deciding requires you to make trade-offs, choosing what to do and what *not* to do.

STEP 4: DESIGN—BUILDING YOUR BRIDGE

It's one thing to think about a bridge. It's another to actually build that bridge. While natural bridges like logs over streams exist, the majority of functional bridges are man-made. The Design step asks you to develop an action plan that will help you reach the goals you've set, using the appropriate resources. Just as a designer creates a blueprint for a bridge, we can design a StrategyPrint for life.

STEP 5: DRIVE—CROSSING YOUR BRIDGE

Once the bridge has been designed and built, the true test begins. Can you move across this bridge, from one side to the other? A bridge that looks good but crumbles when used is of little value. The Drive step guides your actions and moves you forward on a daily basis according to the strategy you have designed. It includes the ability to execute your plan without becoming distracted and taken off task by "urgent" but unimportant things that eat away at your time.

In each chapter you'll see a "Bridge in Progress" sign that features a story from someone who, in building his or her strategy bridge, has faced the challenges related to that step. At the end of each chapter is a section called "Bridgework Ahead," which enables you to follow the steps for building your bridge, or strategy, by completing the exercises described in the chapter. Following the Bridgework Ahead section is a "Construction Summary" that provides a brief review of the key concepts and tools from the chapter.

What is unique about *Strategy for You*? It is built on a set of universal business strategy principles and tools that have been tailored to another purpose: developing strategy for all the areas of your life. Thinking strategically about your life requires a framework, tools, and discipline. I'll provide the first two. Are you ready to bring the third?

STEP 1: DISCOVER

SELECTING YOUR BRIDGE'S LOCATION

*The first step is not forward.
It is knowing the place
from which it is taken.*

The Ponte Vecchio ("old bridge" in Italian) connects the two halves of the walled medieval city of Florence, Italy. Built after the flood of 1177, the bridge was covered with shops and residences. After it was destroyed by a flood in 1333, reconstruction was completed in 1345, and over the centuries the bridge continued to endure the elements, more floods, and war. On August 2, 1944, German bombers destroyed all the bridges in Florence—except for the Ponte Vecchio. It was spared under direct order from Hitler. Why? Because the Ponte Vecchio is more than just a bridge. It's a marketplace, a piazza for mingling, and even a site for a hospital at one end. Some would say it's a microcosm of the city itself. The Ponte Vecchio long ago answered the first question to be asked about any bridge: "Why?"

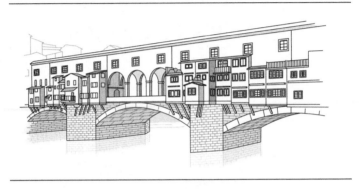

The Ponte Vecchio, Florence, Italy

We can't begin to build a strategy for our lives without first understanding where we are and where we want to go. In order to effectively answer these questions, it's vital to understand where we are starting from. Since people are different, it's reasonable to assume their current situations or starting points will be different as well. That's why books that tout a single formula for success or improvement, without taking into account the different places people are starting from, are worthless. Would you trust a doctor who didn't ask any questions or run any tests to diagnose what was wrong, yet wrote you a prescription anyway? In medicine, the adage is *Prescription without diagnosis equals malpractice.* Before we can "prescribe" strategy, we first need to diagnose the situation—where we stand, where we are today. Before we build our bridge, we first need to identify where we'll be building it.

Surveying the Landscape

When a designer sites the location for a bridge, he makes a survey. A bridge survey is a comprehensive view of the tactical and technical considerations of the proposed bridge. This survey provides critical information about the terrain on which the bridge will start, what direction it will go, and where it will end. The surveyor considers access roads or rails; bridge length; composition and shape of the banks; character of the river, stream, or area to be spanned; and so forth. In essence, the survey is a detailed study of a bridge's beginnings.

In a similar fashion, an Individual Survey provides a visual snapshot of your current situation. It gives a practical means of assessing where you are today by identifying your position in four areas—Mind, Body, Relationships, and Finances. *Mind* consists of all those things that are on your mind: thoughts, feelings, wants, needs, worries, and spirituality. *Body* includes all the elements related to your physical well-being: diet, exercise, age, hobbies, sports, and other lifestyle choices that affect your health. *Relationships* revolve around your connections with family, friends, relatives, coworkers, bosses, neighbors, pets, and so forth. Finally, *Finances* include the things most prominent in terms of your monetary health: job, income, expenses, savings, mortgage, rent, credit card debt, 401(k) plans, children's college funds. Following is an example of an Individual Survey:

Mind

Would like to work from home one day a week

Katie is doing great in school; find ways to challenge her continuing development

What can I do to better position myself for the next promotion?

Find opportunity to volunteer at church

Body

Exercise in morning jump-starts the day

Right shoulder still bothering me

Diet is good at home and bad when I travel

Need four Diet Cokes a day, especially in the afternoon

Waking up 3–4 times a night

Property taxes going up, but house prices still going down

Decide whether to buy or lease next car

No real long-term financial plan

Chris wants to go to Europe for our 15-year anniversary

Need to negotiate for pay increase at work

Katie's screen time keeps increasing

Mom needs full-time care

Not spending much time with friends

Date nights are few but still fun

New coworker is not a team player

Finances

Relationships

Figure 1.1: Individual Survey

The Individual Survey transfers your thoughts and feelings to paper so you can get a better view, or survey, of your life as a whole. Conducting an Individual Survey on a regular basis also gives you a way to track what's changing in your life, so you can factor those changes into your strategies.

According to author Donald Sull, studies of air traffic

controllers have found that up to 70 percent of their mistakes result from an inability to track factors that showed a change in the situation, even though those factors were readily available.[1] To modify a popular saying, if you don't know where you're going, there's a good chance you have no idea where you are in the first place. And if you don't know where your bridge is starting from, it's impossible to stay on top of changes that can have a significant impact on your goals and strategies. Successfully identifying the highlights in your Individual Survey lays the foundation for the ability to choose the right action in the right place at the right time.

Strategy's Destination

Imagine you're driving back from a business meeting and you realize you won't be home in time for dinner. You decide to hit a fast-food drive-thru and grab something to go so you can still get home in time to give the kids a kiss goodnight. Unfortunately, here's how the driver in front of you orders:

> **Drive-thru attendant:** Would you like to try our new hot-'n'-spicy bucket-o'-stuff today?

> **Customer:** Uhhh . . . no thanks. I'm hungry and I'd like some food.

> **Attendant:** Yeah, I kind of figured that, since you're here at a fast-food restaurant. What would you like?

> **Customer:** Well, I like meat. Maybe I'll have some type of meat product.

Attendant: Fantastic. We have about sixty-three meat products on the menu. Can you be a little more specific?

Customer: OK, how about meat with some type of bread?

Attendant: Great, that narrows it down to forty-five meat products that come on some type of bread. Do you want a hamburger, cheeseburger, chicken sandwich, beef sandwich, panini, gyro . . . ? Look, pal, I don't have all night. Do I have to read you the entire menu?

Customer: OK, how about a hamburger?

Attendant: Anything to drink with that?

Customer: Sure. I'll have a beverage.

While this exchange would be ridiculous even by fast-food drive-thru standards, its equivalent happens every day: People go through the motions of their business and personal lives without truly knowing what it is they want. Don't believe me? Stop reading this and go ask five people what their top three goals are for this year. Three out of the five won't know. At least, that's what research conducted with twenty thousand people showed.[2] Most people simply can't articulate what it is that they want to achieve. Their destination is forever unknown.

Ask your spouse, partner, friend, or neighbor what his or her top three goals are for the next year. After the quick-witted

"Win the lottery and quit my job," my guess is he or she won't really have an answer. While it's hard to believe that something so fundamental as goals and objectives can be overlooked, remember that research shows only 15 percent of people take the time to write down what they want (goals) and how they will achieve it (strategy).

This begs the question: Is it really that important to understand the difference between goals, objectives, strategies, and tactics? From a business perspective, the answer is a definitive "yes." A study on financial performance shows that companies with clearly defined and well-articulated strategies coupled with three other primary practices, on average, grow their sales by 32 percent a year and increase their profits by 41.5 percent a year over a ten-year period.[3] How does that compare with your organization's results?

A common response is, "Well, if it weren't for the bad economy, we'd have those numbers too." I hate to burst the *It's not our fault, it's the economy* bubble, but I will. Research by Matthew Olson found that 70 percent of a company's poor performance is due to decisions about strategy, and *only 4 percent* can be attributed to the overall economy.[4] So the next time somebody in your company blames the economy for his or her bad results, smile and hand that person a mirror.

It's common to hear businesspeople blame the economy for their poor performance. As Olson's research shows, however, the real cause of their failure is their inability to develop sound strategy. The same can be said for our personal lives. We all know people who blame external circumstances for their unhappiness or inability to create the life they want. Any of the following statements sound familiar?

> "I can't just quit my job. I have bills to pay, and the job market is still bad."

> "My marriage isn't great because my spouse has changed since we were married."

> "My kids don't understand that I have to be responsive to e-mail and my BlackBerry is the only way to keep up."

> "I'd like to go back to school, but I don't have the time."

> "I'd love to do another type of work, but I can't because I'd have to take a major pay cut."

> "My doctor says I need to lose weight, but she doesn't understand how hard it is to exercise and eat healthfully when you travel as much as I do."

Excuses are a symptom of not having a strategy. You can stand around watching others pursue their dreams, or you can take control of your life and actively build your bridge to a better place. Let's introduce a tool that can replace excuses with strategy.

The GOST Framework

I've developed a simple framework to help people understand the differences between goals, objectives, strategies, and tactics: the GOST Framework.

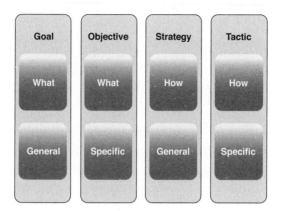

Figure 1.2: The GOST Framework

Say you were using the GOST Framework for an upcoming trip. It might look like this:

Goal	Objective	Strategy	Tactics
Get to Ohio	Arrive at Mom's house by Christmas Eve	Fly	Cab to airport; AA flight departing 2:10 p.m. and arriving 3:45 p.m.; Hertz rental car to Mom's house

GOAL

A goal is a target. It describes what you are trying to achieve—in *general* terms. Examples of goals include the following:

1. Lose weight.

2. Win the quarterly sales contest for my region.

3. Become closer to my spouse or partner.

OBJECTIVE

An objective also describes what you are trying to achieve. The difference is, an objective is what you are trying to achieve in *specific* terms. The common acronym used to help flesh out an objective is SMART: Specific, Measurable, Achievable, Relevant, and Time-bound. Objectives should be all these things, and they should flow directly from the goals you've already set. As you'll see, the objective examples match up with the corresponding goals we established earlier. Examples of objectives include the following:

1. **Goal:** Lose weight.

   Objective: Lose 15 pounds in six months.

2. **Goal:** Win the quarterly sales contest for my region.

   Objective: Achieve $250,000 in sales by the end of the third quarter of this year.

3. **Goal:** Become closer to my spouse or partner.

   Objective: Have a date night with my spouse every week at a new restaurant.

STRATEGY & TACTICS

Once we've identified the goals and objectives, then we can determine the strategy, which is the bridge to achieving them. Strategy and tactics are *how* you will achieve your goals and objectives—how you will allocate your resources to do so. Strategy is the *general* resource allocation plan. The tactics, then, are how *specifically* or tangibly you will do that. Using the previous examples, we can see how the strategy serves as the path to achieving our goals and objectives.

1. **Goal:** Lose weight.

   Objective: Lose 15 pounds in six months.

   Strategy: Eliminate weight-causing behaviors and create weight-reducing behaviors.

   Tactics: Drink diet soda rather than regular soda. Purchase a treadmill and elastic strength bands to exercise at home for thirty minutes a day, five days a week. Go to bed forty minutes earlier and wake up forty minutes earlier to complete exercise in the morning. Eat a protein-based breakfast, choosing from such options as eggs, peanut butter, ham, or a protein shake.

2. **Goal:** Win the quarterly sales contest for my region.

   Objective: Achieve $250,000 in sales by the end of the third quarter of this year.

   Strategy: Focus selling efforts on expanding share of wallet with current customers.

   Tactics: Schedule appointments with my top twenty customers. Prepare a sell sheet showing dollarized value of using our products in combination. Videotape three customers using two or more of our products in combination. Purchase an iPad and put new sell sheets and videos into a presentation for use during customer meetings.

3. **Goal:** Become closer to my spouse or partner.

   Objective: Have a date night with my spouse every week at a new restaurant.

   Strategy: Dedicate thoughtful time to my spouse to rekindle our relationship.

> **Tactics:** Download Urbanspoon app to mobile phone to identify potential restaurants. Build a database of restaurants, including their locations and phone numbers. Create a list of live entertainment establishments, theaters, and other recreational venues. Develop a calendar just for date night, and populate it with choices.

If you're having trouble differentiating between strategy and tactics, you can use the "rule of touch." If you can reach out and physically touch it (e.g., a treadmill, a sell sheet, a calendar), it's a tactic.

It's often said that strategy is long-term and tactics are short-term. In reality, long-term and short-term descriptors for strategy and tactics may or may not apply. A strategy that successfully helps you achieve your goal of losing 15 pounds in six months might be short-term compared to tactics you'll use for years to come in keeping off the unwanted pounds. Using time as the criterion for distinguishing between strategy and tactics is common, but this is the wrong approach.

Since we can't see or physically reach out and touch strategy, it's often skipped in favor of going straight to tactics. Many of the business plans I've reviewed over the past fifteen years list goals first, then objectives, and then tactics. If you don't set strategy before tactics, however, you have no way of intelligently changing course when you're not meeting your objectives. Having a high-performance car (tactic) doesn't help you reach the other side of the river if there isn't a bridge (strategy) to cross it.

With no strategy, you'll fall into a game of "tactical roulette," where you continually chamber a new tactic and pull the trigger. Sooner or later, you'll find yourself looking at a dead plan.

Purpose Channeling

Hello. Do you remember me? I'm your purpose, your reason for being. Once you knew me. Then life got in the way.

After surveying the beginning and end points of your bridge, you can turn your attention to ensuring you're establishing the right bridge in the first place. The most powerful concept in determining the right bridge is purpose. *Purpose* is defined as "the reason for which something exists or is done, made, used, etc." Determining your purpose is critical to long-term success and happiness.

For most people, the largest investment of time is in their work. Yet, as the data presented earlier demonstrates, only 20 percent of adults are in a job that allows them to maximize their potential. Think about your spouse, partner, colleagues, friends, and relatives. How many of them are unhappy with their job, their industry, and maybe even their career? The answer: too many.

Over the past twenty years, I've developed a process for finding one's purpose and creating a link between that purpose and one's work. In fact, I used the process myself fourteen years ago to lead me into the roles I have today: entrepreneur, author, strategist, professor, and speaker. I don't look at it as having a "job." Rather, I have identified my purpose and continually find new outlets in which to use it. The outlets have been both for-profit and not-for-profit, both short-term and long-term.

The common denominator is that these outlets have allowed me to develop, enjoy, and serve my purpose in life. This process is called Purpose Channeling.

In its most basic form, personal purpose can be described as passion plus talent. Purpose Channeling is a process designed to discover the themes present when you've merged passion and talent, and then to develop productive channels for those themes. The channels allow the *what* and the *how* to be individually created so you can tailor them to your purpose.

There are seven stages in the Purpose Channeling process:

1. Ask yourself, *What do I want?*
2. Ask yourself, *How will I know when I get it?*
3. Describe the time frames in your life.
4. Recall moments when you were deeply excited.
5. Determine the themes running through your moments of excitement.
6. Identify potential channels.
7. Prepare your channels.

STAGE 1: ASK YOURSELF, *WHAT DO I WANT?*

The answers to this question flow in and out of our minds every day. Unless we commit to writing them down, however, they don't have any real power. As you think about this question, consider the four areas from the Individual Survey to spark your thoughts—Mind, Body, Relationships, and Finances. What is it that you want in each of these areas? Here are a few of the responses I came up with fourteen years ago.

What do you want?

Mind

> Freedom to do what I want, when I want
>
> Growth in spirituality
>
> Opportunities to speak/perform for others

Body

> Good health
>
> Time to exercise each day
>
> Eating and drinking in moderation

Relationships

> Strong relationships with family and friends
>
> Opportunity to lead and help others
>
> Work with people who are hungry to improve

Finances

> Financial latitude
>
> Influence on big-picture decision-making at work
>
> Entrepreneurial activity

STAGE 2: ASK YOURSELF, *HOW WILL I KNOW WHEN I GET IT?*

One of the things that make each of us unique is the dramatically different interpretation we can have of the same idea. One person's definition of financial independence may be to earn enough money to take a vacation each year, while someone else's definition of financial independence might be to accumulate $50 million and retire by age fifty. We must then give ourselves milestones to gauge our wants from Stage 1.

As you review your responses to Stage 1, consider what it would finally look like to achieve these wants, and then record your ideas here in Stage 2. The following are a sample of my responses.

How will you know when you get it?

Mind

Peace of mind

Presence of God in my life

Engaging, enjoyable work

Meaningful, clearly defined purpose

Time and money allocated to my personal and professional development

Body

Schedule that allows me to exercise on a regular basis

Feeling energized throughout the day

Continually improving cardiovascular conditioning

Increased physical strength sparks a willingness to take risks

Relationships

Family of my own

Learning from coworkers, clients

Able to help those less fortunate

Not missing family commitments because of work

Staying in touch with old friends on a regular basis

Mentally open to making new friends

Finances

Not required to go to an outside office daily

Investment strategy in place

Principal decision maker at a company

Responsibility, risk, and reward all at a high level

Amount of vacation at my discretion

Paychecks signed by me

People/companies are paying to hear me speak

STAGE 3: DESCRIBE THE TIME FRAMES IN YOUR LIFE.

Past behavior is a strong predictor of future behavior. To help us begin uncovering our purpose channels, it's beneficial to look back on our past. In looking back, we're going to identify activities, hobbies, interests, jobs, educational experiences, and other moments that describe specific time periods. The descriptors should cover a range of items, from the seemingly small (fishing with Grandpa) to the big events (your wedding). To complete this stage, you may want to elicit input from family and friends for your earlier years, to help shake the cobwebs from those more distant memories. Consider using time frames such as birth–age 9, ages 10–19, ages 20–29, ages 30–39, ages 40–49, and so on.

So as not to bore you with my life story, I've listed only a handful of items for each time frame as examples.

Time frame descriptions

Birth–age 9

Baptism; playing sports in the backyard with family; soccer team undefeated; first communion; baseball catcher; book reports on UFOs; watching *Scooby-Doo* on Saturday mornings; huge birthday parties with my twenty-five first cousins.

Ages 10–19

Lost student council president election in sixth grade to Amy Phelan; ran for junior high cross-country team conference champions; three grandparents passed away; played goalie on travel soccer team; worked as garbage man during summers throughout high school; played college soccer; taught religious education class; started youth soccer camp during summers throughout college.

Ages 20–29

First job out of college was in sales; ran Chicago Marathon; bungee jumping; serving as Eucharistic minister at church; skydiving; playing tennis with Dad; playing poker with Mom, Dad, and Grandma; completed MBA; mentored disadvantaged kids.

At age thirty, I began developing the Purpose Channeling process, so I used the previous three time frames as the foundation for my channel discovery.

STAGE 4: RECALL MOMENTS WHEN YOU WERE DEEPLY EXCITED.

OK, so maybe my wife wouldn't list me in this section. No matter. Here we're beginning to dig through our past to identify the times when we experienced complete engagement and excitement. Begin looking through the time frame descriptions to jump-start your thinking. In which of the activities, hobbies, jobs, volunteer opportunities, personal moments, and so forth were you fully engaged ("into it")? Which of these experiences did you find exciting and fulfilling?

The following Stage 4 examples are from my experience.

Moments of excitement

Mind

    Delivering the commencement speech at high school graduation

    Teaching religion to children

    Acting in a company skit

Body

    Competing in sports/games: golf, tennis, billiards, basketball, beach volleyball, soccer, poker

    Riding roller coasters

    Skydiving

Relationships

    Mentoring children to learn to read

    Sitting outside on driveway with parents at night and talking about the future

Marrying my wife
Seeing my children being born

Finances
Developing strategy concepts
Reading professional development books
Giving sales skills presentations at work

STAGE 5: DETERMINE THE THEMES RUNNING THROUGH YOUR MOMENTS OF EXCITEMENT.

Once we've created the list of exciting moments, the task now is to pick out themes running through these moments. These themes represent the highlights of engagement and excitement found throughout your life. After several rounds of reviewing and thinking about your Stage 4 moments of excitement list, these themes tend to rise to the surface like bubbles. As they bubble up, jot them down.

Don't feel that this needs to be accomplished in one sitting. The creative process suggests that an incubation period—a time when you aren't consciously focusing on the list—actually helps the process become more fruitful. So put it down, go for a walk, play with the kids, and come back to it later in the week.

Once again, I've provided a few personal examples for your reference, based on the moments I listed in Stage 4.

Themes
Competition
Preparation
Strategic thinking

Risk

Creation

Teaching

Speaking

STAGE 6: IDENTIFY POTENTIAL CHANNELS.

Now that we've homed in on the themes running through your moments of engagement and excitement, we want to explore potential outlets or channels for those themes. A *channel* is defined as "a route through which something progresses." A *route* denotes a course or way of passage. In identifying channels, therefore, we are in effect creating a *course or way of passage* for our inner talents, passions, and dreams to reach the outer world. The word *progresses* in the definition indicates the ability we have to move our lives forward in a significant and compelling way.

Channels may include roles, responsibilities, jobs, vocations, volunteer opportunities, and such. Once you've exhausted your list of potential channels, take this opportune time to get input from other people. Most of us are simply not aware of all the possible channels for a theme, and soliciting the input of others can expand the breadth of the search.

The following are examples of the themes I identified fourteen years ago as I went through this process:

Potential channels

Professor

Professional speaker

Adventure guide

Strategy consultant

Market research facilitator

Writer

Entrepreneur

Actor (I guess Brad Pitt's job is still safe!)

STAGE 7: PREPARE YOUR CHANNELS.

Unless you have a wand, the channels you've selected don't magically appear. Nor does your readiness to enter them. This stage requires research to better understand the channels—their risks, their rewards, and their realities and what it takes to live them. Once you've researched the channels and weighed their pros and cons, you can begin preparing to enter them. As you'll see from the following notes on channel preparation, I began preparing and continued to research several channels that I later decided not to continue along (at least, not at that time).

Channel preparation

Entrepreneur

Completed graduate course in entrepreneurship; studied business planning process; created several business plans based on real-world opportunities. Created own company in 2002 and have developed dozens of proprietary strategy tools, including the StrategyPrint and Strategy Vault tools and the StrategySphereSystem software.

Strategist/professor/author

Worked as a chief strategy officer at a marketing consulting firm, helping companies develop competitive positioning and strategic plans. Completed MBA in management at the Kellstadt Graduate School of Business at DePaul University; completed postgraduate courses on strategy at the University of Chicago Booth School of Business and the Amos Tuck School of Business Administration at Dartmouth College; did fifteen years of research on strategy, reviewing and summarizing hundreds of books and thousands of articles. Spent five years as a professor of management at the Lake Forest Graduate School of Management.

Adventure guide

Earned scuba-diving certification; went on safari in Africa; created workout regimen to raise fitness level.

Professional speaker

Joined National Speakers Association and attended regional and state chapter meetings; attended industry/motivational conferences and took notes on speakers (style, content, platform skills, etc.); took on more presentation roles at current job.

Actor

Completed all five levels of one-year improv program at Second City in Chicago; took acting class; spoke to agents about realities of the business; read books on different acting techniques.

Discovering purpose is the essential starting point. It doesn't matter if you're a twenty-two-year-old college graduate, a fifty-year-old sales manager, or a seventy-five-year-old retiree; finding (or renewing) your purpose will drive your level of happiness, fulfillment, and self-expression. We all have a unique purpose. Have you found yours?

BRIDGE IN PROGRESS

I'm a regional sales manager working for a medical device company. Our region has won the Pinnacle Award for top sales region twice in the past three years, and we consistently exceed our forecasted numbers. I'm a Type A personality who loves to set goals and then work hard to achieve them. I think this is because I grew up with two older brothers and I was always trying to keep up with them.

On one of my many business trips about six months ago, I was sitting in my hotel room checking e-mail around ten o'clock at night, and I hit a wall. I realized my short-term, numbers-oriented approach at work was exactly the same approach I took with the rest of my life. While I was excelling at work, there wasn't much else going on in my life. I started to think about what my life would look like in five years, and other than my job, I really didn't have any idea what to work toward.

On the plane ride home the next day, I sat with a pen and paper and thought about what I wanted the rest of my life to look like. Better relationships and a more defined purpose were the two things that stood out. I decided to invest time in reconnecting with friends and to dedicate more time on the weekends to doing fun things with my husband. When I thought about my purpose, I kept coming back to setting and achieving goals. I was good at that and enjoyed the constant challenge.

A few weeks later, one of the friends I reconnected with mentioned a group she was volunteering with called REACH. The program matches students with sponsors who act as mentors and also finance the student's four-year private high school education. The group's mission is "to provide opportunities for at-risk youth to achieve academic and personal success through a quality, values-based education and the guidance of caring adult mentors." REACH has provided scholarships and mentoring services to nearly two hundred at-risk youth in the community since its inception nearly ten years ago. To date, eighty-seven youth have graduated from the program, and more than 90 percent of them have gone on to attend college. Since 2005, 100 percent of the graduates have been accepted to college.

I went to several REACH meetings, and today I head up sponsor recruitment. It's been a great chance for me to use my purpose to help others.

—Jennifer S.

Mission Statement

Once you've identified your purpose and potential channels, you've uncovered where you are going and *why.* Understanding *why* is perhaps the most motivating and success-driving reason for realizing your full potential.

In business, *why* takes the form of a mission statement. A mission is a clear, concise, and enduring statement of the reasons for an organization's existence. A mission statement directly or indirectly answers five questions:

1. *What* do you do?
2. *How* do you do it?
3. *Whom* are you serving?
4. *Why* are you doing it?
5. What's *different?*

Having completed the Purpose Channeling exercise, you can use the themes you identified in Stage 5 to work on crafting your individual Mission Statement. In the exercise from earlier, my themes from Stage 5 were competition, preparation, strategic thinking, risk, creation, teaching, and speaking. Therefore, my individual Mission Statement (always a work in progress!) looks like this:

> I seek to grow as a family member, friend, and business leader by *thinking strategically*; by investing time in thinking about what's most important to the people in my life; and by using my talents to help them

reach their goals. I will both teach and learn from people how to continually generate new insights to fulfill our personal and professional purposes. I believe we must outthink to outperform, compete to excel, and plan to succeed.

An individual Mission Statement can help you stay focused on what's important in your life. It can also serve as a strategic filter to help you make better decisions. If an opportunity supports your individual mission, then it's a wise choice. If the opportunity doesn't support the mission, then it's a *no*.

Vision Statement

While a mission statement helps you focus on your current purpose, a vision statement represents your *future* purpose. It represents a mental picture of what you aspire to be. The vision provides strategic guidance and motivational focus. As you progress across your bridges or strategies toward your goals, the vision acts as a lighthouse to help you continuously stay on course. Whereas the mission statement represents the purpose being lived out today, the vision statement represents the future purpose still to be achieved. It's the ultimate person you aspire to be. If a goal is what you want to achieve, the vision is what you want to be.

While an organization's vision statement represents a collective whole, the individual Vision Statement is often written for a specific area of one's life, such as Mind or Finances. It can be equally powerful, however, in the areas of Body and

Relationships. Here are several examples of individual Vision Statements.

Mind
Become a leader in the national awareness and prevention of child abuse.

Body
Be as healthy at age seventy-five as you are at age forty-five.

Relationships
Be the central link in the extended family to help maintain connections with your relatives around the world.

Finances
Generate enough wealth to buy a small island.

Remember, the Vision Statement requires you to think big, dream big, and define what you aspire to be.

Values List

Ingrained in the current and future purpose are values—the ideals and principles that guide your thoughts and behavior. Because values represent your core beliefs, they are a powerful shaper of your strategies. Values influence the decisions you make, the attitude you carry, how you interact with others, and inevitably, who you are as a person. They provide a benchmark in your daily decisions, because your chosen course of action must match up with your values in order to be considered good decisions. Each person has a unique set of values, based on numerous factors that might include family, friends, upbringing, religion, and personality.

As with purpose or mission, the strength and effect of values depend on how deeply you believe in them and your ensuing commitment to them. One of the common mistakes in identifying one's values is to list terms that are honorable (e.g., generous, caring, honest) but not really those you hold most deeply. It's helpful to list those values that are most important to you and that give you your unique character. A useful set of values meets certain criteria: It represents your ideals and principles; it guides your actions and decisions; it provides a foundation for your mission and vision; and it is true to you.

The following are a sample of individual values that you might choose to populate your Values List:

Optimism	Love
Thoughtfulness	Hope
Risk	Generosity
Practicality	Strength
Helpfulness	Service
Creativity	Freedom
Intelligence	Expertise
Sensitivity	Competition
Responsiveness	Equality
Drive	Sustainability
Passion	

As you consider your values, think about the company you work for and the community or church groups you belong to, and ask how similar these organizations' values are to yours.

INDIVIDUAL SURVEY

Develop your Individual Survey by identifying and recording the highlights in each of the four areas (Mind, Body, Relationships, Finances). As you work through this exercise, it can be eye-opening to get feedback from coworkers, family members, and friends on how they perceive the key points in each of those areas for you.

CREATING YOUR GOST FRAMEWORK

Use the following process to help you develop an understanding of your goals, objectives, strategies, and tactics:

1. Identify your top three *goals* and write them down.

2. Just below the goals you recorded, write down your top three *objectives*. Each objective should directly relate to one goal.

3. Now create *strategies* and *tactics* to reach the goals and objectives you listed earlier, and write them down. Each strategy and tactic should directly relate to a corresponding goal and objective.

PURPOSE CHANNELING

Complete the following seven-stage Purpose Channeling exercise to determine the ideal outlets for your purpose:

1. Ask yourself, *What do I want?*

2. Ask yourself, *How will I know when I get it?*

3. Describe the time frames in your life (birth–age 9, ages 10–19, etc.)

4. Recall moments when you were deeply excited.

5. Determine the themes running through your moments of excitement.

6. Identify potential channels.

7. Prepare your channels.

MISSION STATEMENT

Using the themes from Stage 5 of the Purpose Channeling exercise, craft an individual Mission Statement. The statement should directly or indirectly address the following five questions:

1. *What* do you do?

2. *How* do you do it?

3. *Whom* are you serving?

4. *Why* are you doing it?

5. What's *different?*

VISION STATEMENT

Building on your current purpose, or Mission Statement, now think about what your purpose will look like five, ten, fifteen, or even twenty-five years from now. Start by writing down what you'd like to be, using the four areas of Mind, Body, Relationships, and Finances as a guide. The Vision Statement can be specific to one of those areas or can represent your overall future purpose. It should align with your strategies and your current purpose, and it should provide you with the motivational boost you need to get excited about the journey. The important thing is to dream big.

VALUES STATEMENT

Begin by creating a laundry list of the traits or characteristics that you believe best describe you. Ask others around you—people you trust—what they perceive to be the values that best describe you. Once you've developed a comprehensive list, begin to whittle it down to approximately five values that you truly believe represent you and who you want to continue to be. This is your Values Statement.

CONSTRUCTION SUMMARY

As you move through life and your goals evolve, so too must your strategies. New bridges will be built for new challenges.

The Individual Survey is a practical tool for assessing where you are today by identifying the highlights or key happenings in four areas: Mind, Body, Relationships, and Finances.

The GOST Framework lays out the following elements:

1. Goal: What you are trying to achieve in *general* terms
2. Objective: What you are trying to achieve in *specific* terms
3. Strategy: How you will achieve your goal (*generally*)
4. Tactic: How you will achieve your goal (*specifically*)

Purpose is defined as "the reason for which something exists or is done, made, used, etc." Perhaps the biggest reason many people are on the "bridge to nowhere" is that they haven't really considered their purpose—their reason for being. To help you determine your purpose, you can follow the seven steps in the Purpose Channeling process:

1. Ask yourself, *What do I want?*
2. Ask yourself, *How will I know when I get it?*

3. Describe the time frame in your life.

4. Recall moments when you were deeply excited.

5. Determine the themes running through your moments of excitement.

6. Identify potential channels.

7. Prepare your channels.

A mission is a clear, concise, and enduring statement of the reasons for an organization's existence. A Mission Statement can provide you with a constant reminder of your purpose and can ensure that your decisions are helping you live it.

A Mission Statement directly or indirectly answers five questions:

1. *What* do you do? (What?)

2. *How* do you do it? (How?)

3. *Whom* are you serving? (Who?)

4. *Why* are you doing it? (Why?)

5. What's *different*? (Uniqueness?)

A Vision Statement represents your future purpose, creating a mental picture of what you aspire to be.

Values are the core beliefs, ideals, and principles that guide your thoughts and behavior.

STEP 2: DIFFERENTIATE

IMAGINING YOUR BRIDGE'S STYLE

No two are alike.
Therein lies the value.
The challenge is to embrace it.

In the world of bridge design, where thousands of highly skilled professionals work, names like John Roebling, Joseph Strauss, and Santiago Calatrava stand out—not because they created structures similar to those of their colleagues, but rather for their visionary and differentiated styles.

John Roebling conceived the Brooklyn Bridge in 1855 and received approval to build in June 1869. Unfortunately, due to an accident on June 28, 1869, in which a ferry crushed his foot, Roebling died from tetanus a few weeks later. Remarkably, his son Washington and daughter-in-law Emily saw the project through to completion for the famous bridge's opening on May 23, 1883. With its heavy Gothic portals and aerial web of cables, the Brooklyn Bridge brought together the New York City boroughs of Brooklyn and Manhattan—physically, socially, and historically. To this day, the Brooklyn Bridge is a distinctive American emblem that has inspired writers, artists, and people from all walks of life. The Roeblings' innovative style embodied the strength, determination, and relentless pursuit of the improbable that capture the city's persona.

The Brooklyn Bridge, New York City, New York

On the opposite side of the country, Joseph Strauss eagerly embraced the challenge of connecting Marin County and the city of San Francisco by spanning the Golden Gate Strait. The path was not easy; his initial design was ridiculed as "an upside-down rat-trap," but he was so consumed with achieving his vision of spanning the crossing that he reluctantly passed along design duties to Charles Alton Ellis, a professor of structural and bridge engineering at the University of Illinois. Enduring the Great Depression and more than 2,300 legal disputes by the Southern Pacific Railroad, which owned the ferries transporting two million riders a year across the strait, Strauss broke ground on the Golden Gate Bridge on January 5, 1933.

The Golden Gate Bridge, San Francisco, California

By its opening on May 28, 1937, the Art Deco–inspired towers in the stepped-back pyramid style of the Mayan culture grew to 746 feet above the roadway—at the time, the highest bridge towers in the world. Completing the distinctive look of this icon, which the American Society of Civil Engineers ranks as one of the Seven Wonders of the Modern World, is its color:

International Orange. The reddish, lead-based primer initially used to protect the structure from the weather was a serendipitous, inspired choice—both a perfect blend with the Marin headlands and an important navigational contrast with the gray-blue sky and water. While this uncommon and beautiful color seemed predestined, keep in mind that the US Air Force wanted the entire Golden Gate Bridge painted with orange and white stripes, while the Navy was pushing for black and yellow stripes!

More recently, Spanish architect, designer, and engineer Santiago Calatrava has advanced the concept of bridge design once again. Though he has designed dozens of bridges around the world, perhaps his most notable is the cable-stayed Puente del Alamillo in Seville, Spain. The 656-foot structure is suspended by thirteen twin cables, forming a 466-foot steel tower angled backward at 58 degrees. In reviewing Santiago Calatrava's many stunning works, architecture professor Alexander Tzonis wrote, "Calatrava used . . . the strategy of optimizing structure through *differentiation* [emphasis added] and profiling of the most distinguished element of the project."[1] Calatrava's unique style is a culmination of his expertise in the fields of engineering, architecture, and design. His bridges are different in a most compelling way.

Each day, too many of us strive for a life of mediocrity and unfulfilled potential—at least, that's what our behavior indicates. We do the same things in the same ways as everyone else, and then we wonder why we haven't found success and happiness. We conform to standards at work, at school, in the neighborhood, and within society as a whole. Instead of seeking out ways to positively differentiate ourselves, we see our social activities, entertainment preferences, and PowerPoint presentations at work looking more and more similar to those of the people around us. If familiarity breeds contempt, similarity breeds apathy.

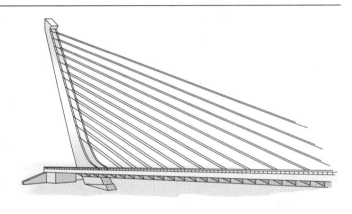

The Puente Alamillo, Seville, Spain

From an early age, we're expected to conform, blend in, and behave like others. Instead of a fertile environment within which we can cultivate our own style, we experience wave after wave of signals that it's safer to follow the pack—even if that pack is headed over a cliff. But the people who have reached the pinnacles of success in their field, like the visionary bridge builders mentioned here, have been very different from those around them.

Deviation from the Norm

The world of entertainment provides many examples of the positive effect of embracing your own style. Johnny Cash is a musician whose career popularity spanned more than fifty years, not because he was a better singer than his contemporaries, but because he had a distinctive voice and wrote songs that were true to him. Dressed all in black, Cash sang of how life can harden a man over time yet offered hope that redemption can be found. Today, musicians such as Eminem and Lady Gaga have broken through the clutter in similar fashion, thanks to their ability to blend vocal talent with their individualistic personas.

Perhaps one of the best examples of the qualitative and financial power of differentiation comes from the movie industry. Consider *Toy Story; Toy Story 2; Toy Story 3; Monsters, Inc.; A Bug's Life; Finding Nemo; The Incredibles; Cars; Cars 2; Ratatouille; WALL-E;* and *Up*. If you have your own kids, grandchildren, or nieces and nephews, there's a good chance you've seen one or more of these dazzling films. Together, they have garnered dozens of Academy Awards and have rung up worldwide sales of nearly $7 billion. What's more amazing is that they have all been created by one company: Pixar. Here's Pixar president Ed Catmull on the importance of differentiation to Pixar's unparalleled success in animated film:

> We as executives have to resist our natural tendency to avoid or minimize risks, which of course is much easier said than done. In the movie business this instinct leads executives to choose to copy successes

> rather than try to create something brand-new. That's why you see so many movies that are so much alike. It also explains why a lot of films aren't very good. If you want to be original, you have to accept the uncertainty, even when it's uncomfortable, and have the capability to recover when your organization takes a big risk and fails.[2]

In order to realize our full potential, we must embrace the style that makes us unique—whatever it might be. Is our style quiet and introverted, or outgoing and extroverted? Do we thrive in an orderly, structured arena, or one that is constantly changing and requires a great deal of flexibility and improvisation? As the examples—both bridges and films—demonstrate, success goes to those who are willing to be different in ways that bring value to others.

Excellence, by its very definition, is *deviation from the norm.* The *norm* is an average, or a standard level. It's where the majority of people wind up, even though there is no such thing as a "normal" human being. Everyone has a unique style built on differences in background, abilities, temperament, and so forth. The difficult thing is uncovering and living that unique style. Despite the difficulty, though, being true to yourself and building a "bridge" that reflects your style will get you where you want to go.

A manager whose products and services represent the norm for the industry may break even or make a modest profit. A person who lives by following the herd, and who is not willing to take the risks that will let his or her true gifts shine through, may be comfortable. But neither will ever know the exhilaration of finding what differentiates them and letting authenticity drive their individual success. We are all different from one another; our bridges, or strategies, need to be different as well.

BRIDGE IN PROGRESS

I'm an associate director of training and development for a large retailer. I help put together and then facilitate training classes on a variety of topics, including customer service, coaching, persuasive communication, and emotional intelligence. Due to the recession, our department has laid off more than half our group. I'm basically doing the work of three people, and I started to feel as if I were running out of gas. I was barely able to keep up, and because I have to cover so many different topics, I knew I wasn't doing as good a job as I was capable of. I felt as though people weren't seeing me at my best because of the situation I've been put in. I'm one of many in a big company, and I didn't feel I had any control over what was happening. It was kind of like treading water, and I didn't know how much longer I could stay afloat.

The turning point for me came when I was coaching my son's baseball team this past spring. I love baseball and working with the kids to improve. After one of the games, my wife, Karen, said on the ride home, "You know, Mike, you do such a great job coaching the kids. I can see how much fun you're having. I wish you came home from work looking like that."

I thought about what she said. I guess one of the reasons I enjoy baseball so much is that it's a game, and we all love games. I also put a ton of time into watching, studying, and reading about the game. I decided to see if I could make what I do at work more fun. So for each of the topics I teach, I made up games to help people learn the material. Since coaching in business is a hot topic, I put together the material as I would for coaching a sports team: playbook, "highlights reel" DVD of do's and don'ts, practice schedule, skills and drills, and so on. So far, it's been a big hit. I've even had trainers from other regions come and sit in on my sessions. I finally feel as though I'm differentiating myself, and best of all, I'm enjoying my work more.

—Mike P.

Better or Different?

Consider where you work. Is your product or service *better* than the competition's? Hopefully you're saying to yourself, "Rich, you lovable, laughable fool! That's the wrong question." The real question is, what is the differentiated value you provide to customers?

Here's a newsflash—there is no "better." The term *better* is subjective. Is blueberry pie *better* than banana cream? It depends on whom you ask. However, we can say blueberry pie is *different* because it contains blueberries, which have antioxidants, which are good for you and may help you live longer.

According to research by Bernd Wirtz published in *Long Range Planning,* "Product differentiation, the dimension with the second-highest impact (behind proactiveness) on business performance, strongly hints to the importance of the product portfolio by highlighting the unique features and superior quality of the company's offerings."[3] Translation: Having products or services that provide differentiated value is critical to the long-term success of your business.

Echoing that premise, Harvard Business School professor Michael Porter has said, "There is no best auto company; there is no best car. You're really competing to be unique."[4] The Ford Transit Connect is a prime example. Sporting a European delivery van appearance, it's different from both typical minivans and sport utility vehicles (SUVs). It has 135.3 cubic feet of cargo room behind the front seats, which minivans don't come close to matching, while large SUVs like the Chevy Tahoe top out at only 108.9 cubic feet. It has vanlike side doors and boasts a 6'6" interior height, compared to the six-passenger Mazda5 with an interior height of only 5'3". In its first year on the North American market, the Transit Connect was awarded North American Truck of the Year 2010 at the North American International

Auto Show. Is it the best vehicle out there? Depends on whom you ask. Is it different in ways people value? Absolutely.

If while reading this you've developed a hankering for potato skins and fake ferns, by chance, then we're both thinking Bennigan's. Unfortunately, it's more difficult to find one these days after the parent company filed for Chapter 7 bankruptcy. The reason: The Bennigan's menu and atmosphere failed to differentiate the chain from T.G.I. Friday's, Chili's, and other casual dining restaurants. Bennigan's simply stopped bringing differentiated value to the dining public.

Contrast this with Medieval Times, a castle hosting a jousting tournament while patrons gobble up tomato bisque, a whole roasted chicken, garlic bread, and a potato—with their hands. It may be the one place to eat in America where you can actually encourage your kids to scream during dinner and call the food server "wench." (By the way, this is not recommended the following night at home.) Medieval Times is now regarded as North America's longest-running and most popular dinner attraction, with more than forty million guests having experienced the dinner. This is an example of differentiated value: Medieval Times has differentiated itself from the common experience of dining to ignite business growth.

We can view strategy through two lenses: performing activities that are different from others or performing similar activities in a different way than others do. The difference may seem subtle at first. Here's an example of the first strategy: When Netflix launched, it provided a different activity from the competition—the ability to rent DVDs online. Instead of you going to the video store, the video store came to you—a differentiated activity that provided the value of convenience to customers.

Use the second lens to view the strategy of Enterprise Rent-A-Car. The company performs the same activity as Hertz, Avis, and its other competitors: car rental. However, Enterprise has used different ways of doing it. Historically, it has focused offices in communities, with 5,399 local market offices accounting for 91 percent of all offices, and airport locations, which account for only 9 percent of its offices.

Enterprise is also known for hiring recent college graduates versus experienced managers. It has kept customer service in-house versus outsourcing, and as the ads chorus, Enterprise will come and "pick you up." The result: Enterprise has become the largest car rental company in the United States, because it performs a common activity in ways that are different from the competition.

What all these examples have in common is the emphasis on differentiation for success. Yet the key is not to be different just for the sake of being different. The key is to differentiate in ways that we and others value. Naturally, you share many similarities with family, friends, neighbors, and coworkers. Any organizations you belong to—church, civic groups, companies, charities, school board—are chosen precisely because you have similar beliefs, ideas, and values as others. It is important, though, to add a layer onto these similarities. By adding your unique style, you bring value to yourself and others in different ways. By allowing for the blossoming of these differences, the sum total of your group's contributions is greater than the contribution of any one individual.

Now let's examine how we can use the principle of differentiation in our strategy to continue building a bridge to the life we want.

The Bridge Not Taken

Poet Robert Frost may be best known for his poem "The Road Not Taken," which compares a life in the mainstream with the less worn path he has chosen, and points out the difference it has made. Frost said, "The best things and the best people rise out of their separateness." A literal example of that "rising" follows below.

On August 7, 1974, an extraordinary feat of individual differentiation was displayed. Philippe Petit, a young Frenchman, stepped out on a high wire illegally set up between the twin towers of New York City's World Trade Center, which at the time were the world's tallest buildings. For nearly an hour, Petit walked, danced, and lay on the high wire as it swayed 1,350 feet above the streets of Manhattan. With no safety line of any type, Petit dazzled onlookers below in what became known as "the artistic crime of the century."

This magnificent spectacle, captured in the 2008 Academy Award–winning documentary *Man on Wire*, was a brilliant display of how we can leave our own mark on the world. Petit took a not-so-different activity like walking and made it completely his own with the grand vision of walking through the sky between the two highest buildings in the world. Not to be confused with a lark, his adventure was preceded by six years of planning and preparation. He literally created a bridge between two architectural and now, sadly, lost icons.

And as with any truly great strategy, Petit's required taking risks. In order to realize true differentiation, he faced potential imprisonment and accepted the greatest risk of all: death. When you are walking on a wire 1,350 feet above the pavement with no safety line, one unexpected gust of wind could end both your adventure and your life. Petit took that risk and was successful. His individual strategy differentiated him from all others and cemented his legacy.

As noted earlier, strategy can be viewed as either performing similar activities in different ways from others (as Petit did) or performing different activities than others do. British artist Damien Hirst has taken a dramatic approach to art by performing it in a different way. He created a series of artworks in which dead animals (including a shark, a sheep, and a cow) are preserved—sometimes after having been dissected—in formaldehyde. While his artwork—such as *The Physical Impossibility of Death in the Mind of Someone Living*, featuring a shark in a tank of formaldehyde—has caused great debate on what is or is not art, one thing can't be denied: his ability to differentiate himself and his work through a well-conceived strategy that has jolted the business world of art. Hirst's different artistic activity has propelled him to become reportedly Britain's richest living artist, with his wealth valued at nearly $350 million.

While Hirst employed different activities in the world of art, award-winning chef Grant Achatz has taken the common activity of cooking and is transforming it in different ways. Named the 2008 top chef in the United States by the James Beard

Foundation, he is the owner of Alinea, *Restaurant* magazine's best restaurant in North America in 2011. Now Achatz has conceived a new concept. His latest restaurant, Next, serves four menus per year, from great moments in culinary history or the future, such as Paris 1912, Sicily 1949, and Hong Kong 2036. Instead of reservations, bookings are made more like those for a play or a sporting event. Tickets are fully inclusive of all charges, including service. Ticket price depends on which seating you buy: Saturday at 8 p.m. is more expensive than Wednesday at 9:30 p.m. Wine and beverage pairings begin at a $25 supplement. Next also offers an annual subscription to all four menus at a discount, with preferred seating. The goal is to take diners on a journey through the foods Achatz finds exciting, delicious, and important. He has taken the common activity of running a restaurant and is constantly finding new ways to do it differently. As *Chicago Tribune* food critic Phil Vettel wrote, "Indeed, what Achatz and company have done is reframe the dining experience as a form of repertory theatre."[5]

The Different Value Matrix

Determining how we are different in ways that are valuable to ourselves and others can be a challenging task. To jump-start the process, you can use a tool called the Different Value Matrix (figure 2.1 on the next page) to begin identifying what your differentiating value may be. Use a simple 2 × 2 matrix. The vertical axis is *Value,* from low (bottom) to high (top); the horizontal axis is *Differentiation,* from low (left) to high (right). A list of the individual's knowledge, skills, activities, characteristics, and traits is developed for plotting in the matrix. Once the list is developed, each item is then placed in the matrix according to its value to others (from low to high) and differentiation from others (from low to high).

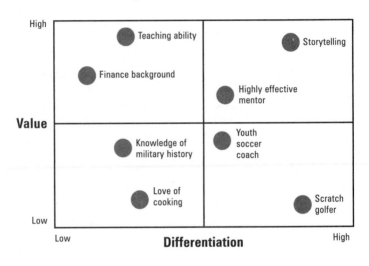

Figure 2.1: Different Value Matrix

In this example, we can see several themes emerge around teaching (mentor, coach) and strategy (military history, finance, golf). We can then consider how to potentially move some of our knowledge and skills into the upper-right quadrant of high value and high differentiation. Perhaps we can develop a training program for new finance managers that integrates examples from military history and uses storytelling to relate current case studies to the managers' roles and responsibilities.

Differentiation will drive success in both your business and your personal life if you have the courage to let the world see what it is that differentiates you. Your individual uniqueness won't appeal to everyone. You must decide who will value it the most. The next step, Step 3: Decide, will show you how.

To begin considering how you are unique, answer the following questions:

1. What are the activities I perform that are truly different from those others perform?

2. What are the similar activities I perform in different ways than others do?

3. What characteristics or traits do I have that are unique to me?

4. What resources do I have that are different from those of others?

5. How does my purpose differ from that of others?

6. How do my family, friends, and colleagues describe my differences?

7. How do my purpose channel themes differ from those of others?

8. In what ways can I express my strategic themes differently than others do?

9. How does my personal development plan differ from that of others?

10. What is the primary differentiated value I bring to people in my life?

Complete a Different Value Matrix using the following steps:

1. List your knowledge, skills, activities, characteristics, and traits.

2. Plot each of these items on the matrix.

3. Identify the items in the highly different, highly valued quadrant (upper right).

4. Consider which items not currently in the upper-right quadrant could, with an investment of your resources, be moved there.

CONSTRUCTION SUMMARY

In order to realize your full potential, you must embrace the things that make you unique. While similarities attract us to many of the groups we belong to, it's our unique talents added to others' unique talents that result in the most value.

Excellence is *deviation from the norm*. If we don't provide ourselves with opportunities to accentuate our authenticity, we deprive the people in our lives from seeing our true selves and prevent reaching our full potential.

When considering your business or individual strategy, there are two lenses through which to view it:

1. Performing different activities than others do
2. Performing similar activities in a different way than others do

Doing the same things in the exact same ways as everyone else may be comfortable and easy, but it's seldom the way to provide the most value to ourselves and others.

The Different Value Matrix is a tool for plotting your knowledge, skills, activities, characteristics, and traits to determine where your focus should be. It asks you to evaluate how relevant and how unique your attributes are in helping you reach the goals you've set.

STEP 3: DECIDE

CHOOSING YOUR
BRIDGE'S MATERIALS

A simple yes here,
a simple no there.
Before long, a life has been lived.

S everal years ago, while my wife, Anne, and I were on safari in Africa, we took a tour of a Maasai Mara tribal village, led by a native guide. He said, "The tribal leader in this village has seven wives because the women in the village do most of the work, from washing clothes in the stream to building the huts that you see out of sticks and cow dung."

When we were finishing up the tour, the tribal leader emerged from his hut and began talking with some of the tourists. As we were about to leave, I noticed the tribal leader talking to Anne and wandered over to eavesdrop on the end of their conversation. This is what he said to her: "We have much work to do here, but our lives are simple and good. I am always looking for the right people to carry on our traditions. I find you to be attractive and sturdy. Would you like to be one of my wives?"

After a long pause (perhaps a little too long for my liking), Anne said, "Well, I love the land here, and the animals are certainly beautiful, but seeing as how I am already married, I'll respectfully have to pass."

On the bouncy jeep ride back to camp, I couldn't let that conversation go without a little jab. So I said, "You know, honey, it sounds like your decision earlier boiled down to me or a house of cow dung."

My wife replied, "Yes, and it was much closer than you think."

In business, as in our personal lives, we are constantly faced with trade-offs. Trade-offs involve incompatible activities: More of one thing means less of another. When we make trade-offs, inherently we're making decisions. The word *decision* comes from the Latin word *decidere*, which means "to cut off." If you have trees on your property, you know that every few years you need to cut off the dead branches or prune the lower ones. Why? To promote new growth.

This principle of pruning for new growth also applies to our individual strategies. When we make decisions, it's often assumed we're simply choosing what to do. But as highly successful individuals and companies have shown, effective strategy is just as much about what you choose *not to do*.

In the process of building a bridge, the designer is faced with thousands of decisions, ranging from the types of materials to use to the most effective style of bridge to employ. Throughout this process, the design, engineering, and building teams are tasked at each turn with optimally using their resources to create a functional and cost-effective structure. In a similar way, you are faced with thousands of decisions in your personal and professional lives. How effectively and efficiently you use your resources—time, talent, and money—will go a long way in deciding your level of fulfillment in life. One of the keys to making these decisions successfully is your ability to focus.

Once you *discover* (Step 1) what your purpose and goals are, and after assessing how you are *different* (Step 2) in ways people value, it's time to *decide* (Step 3) how you're going to use your resources. As we discussed earlier, strategy is defined as the plan for using your resources—time, talent, and money—to achieve your goals. Here in Step 3, the decisions of what to do—and just as important, what *not to do*—are made.

Investing in Your Bridge

One of the most famous movies involving a bridge is the 1957 Academy Award winner for best picture, *The Bridge on the River Kwai*. Based on a true World War II incident, the film recounts the events leading up to British bombers' destruction of two railway bridges built over the Kwai by Allied prisoners of war.

The Japanese Imperial Army's goal was to connect Bangkok and Rangoon (now Yangon) by employing the POWs to cut a 250-mile track through dense jungle by hand.

While the Allied POWs were building a bridge for the enemy, they maintained their focus on restoring their dignity and preserving their will to live by accomplishing a daunting task. Their absolute focus saved their lives. They used the resources available to them (time and talent) to achieve their goal of maintaining their sanity and pride while facing great adversity. Even today, the movie holds up as an exciting and well-told story about the power of planning, focus, and perseverance in an extreme situation.

Imagine for a moment that your life is a movie. How would the audience react? Would they leave halfway through because nothing interesting is happening? Would they criticize your unwillingness to take risks, to make tough decisions? Would they boo if you quit pursuing your goals when the first obstacle got in your way? Would they be pulling for you? Would they cheer your actions, your decisions, and your ability to make something from nothing?

Walking around with the attitude that your course in life is pretty much set and things really won't change for the better is like assuming the last scene of a movie will be the same as the first. Changing your life, changing your attitude, and changing your destiny all are rooted in changing your behavior. And you can change your behavior by changing the way you invest your time and talent.

While some people may keep a sharp eye on how their resources are spent at work, that discipline seems to fly out the window somewhere along the ride home at night. As the research cited earlier confirmed, while 82 percent of executives have a written plan for their business, only 22 percent also have one for their personal life. It's not common to think of how we invest the resources of time, talent, and money in our individual lives, but it can make a big difference in our productivity, fulfillment, and happiness.

If you completed the Bridgework Ahead exercises in Step 1 (Discover) and Step 2 (Differentiate), you have an excellent head start in determining what you should and shouldn't be doing with your time, talent, and money. Identifying the key themes in your life and the purpose channels in which to further explore them is a solid foundation for marking the boundaries of shoulds and shouldn'ts.

BRIDGE IN PROGRESS

I am a strategic and goal-oriented person, and when I completed my master's degree at the University of Michigan, I felt a great sense of accomplishment. As I started my new hospital administrative position, I was ready to take on the world! Even though it had taken me ten years to work and complete my undergraduate degrees and graduate degree, I was already thinking about my next step: getting my doctoral degree, which was, of course, in my plan.

Then I met my husband and was swept off my feet, which was obviously not in the plan. This is where the concepts of focus and flexibility come in. I knew it was time to readjust my long-held plans for this exciting new chapter in my life. My husband and I got married and lived overseas, providing us the opportunity to travel the world. One day early in our marriage, my husband said he felt bad about being "an interruption in my strategic plan." I laughed and assured him that was not the case, although I had not yet completed my dream of getting my doctorate.

Life demands flexibility, just as a business strategy needs to adapt to changing environmental conditions. I eventually completed my PhD, which was very rewarding. I was in my fifties when I crossed that stage to get my diploma, and it was a dream come true. I have been happily married now for thirty years, and I have had a career noted by many achievements, so I would call that a successful implementation of a strategic plan—with some adaptations as required.

—Kathy M.

Before we decide what to say "no" to, it's helpful to understand what we're doing in the first place—and to what extent. In other words, in what areas are you currently investing resources in order to reach your goals? There are several tools that can help us effectively navigate our decisions.

Resource Inventory

The Resource Inventory gives us a means of determining what resources we currently have at our disposal. This is an important first step in eventually mapping out where we're investing these resources and to what degree. By creating a resource inventory that considers the three resource categories of time, talent, and finances, you will be identifying what you have to work with in order to achieve your goals and objectives.

The following is an example of a Resource Inventory:

Time (168 hours in a week)
45 hours at work
16 hours watching TV
3 hours exercising
7½ hours commuting
56 hours sleeping
6 hours with kids
10 hours at meals
6½ hours on computer/phone
7 hours bathing/dressing/etc.
2 hours playing guitar
3 hours on household chores
6 hours coaching youth baseball

Talent
Coaching kids
Mentoring at work
Leading team exercises
Six Sigma Black Belt
Playing guitar

Finances
Combined annual salaries of $156,000
Mortgage of $275,000
Monthly car payment of $320
Kids' 529 college fund of $22,000
Checking account balance of $6,472
Savings account balance of $11,588
Credit card debt of $21,220

Figure 3.1: Resource Inventory

Perhaps one of the most eye-opening aspects of the Resource Inventory exercise comes from carrying a small notebook with you for a week to record how much time you spend on each of your activities. With only 168 hours in a week, it becomes clear how wasting a few hours every week can quickly add up to a half-lived life.

Strategy Profile

Once you've used the Resource Inventory to identify the resources you have to work with, you can begin to evaluate how you're investing those resources. The Strategy Profile is a valuable tool for visualizing your overall strategy. It sheds light on where you're investing your time, talent, and money. In business, it's used to help companies understand where they have differentiated resource allocation, and it often sounds a warning that they are becoming a commodity. A business investing the same level of resources in the same areas as the competition will have a Strategy Profile that mirrors the competition, reflecting a potentially fatal lack of differentiation.

The following is an example of a Strategy Profile. We can see in which areas the person is investing resources and to what extent.

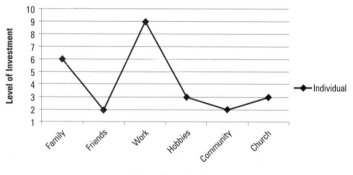

Figure 3.2: Strategy Profile

In this Strategy Profile, it's evident that the majority of this person's resources, especially time and talent, are being invested at work. This is a fairly typical profile in that people considered full-time workers are investing forty-plus hours a week at work, not including commute time, at-home work, reading and answering e-mail, and so forth. The question is, are we satisfied with the Strategy Profile we have? Is this person happy with his or her minimal investment in friends, hobbies, community, and church? Each person will need to determine that for him- or herself.

The Strategy Profile also can be completed for more specific areas of your life. Pick a topic, such as family, and then identify the specific areas of investment, such as spouse, kids, parents, siblings, recreation, vacations, and sports. Then determine how much of your resources (time, talent, finances) you're investing in each of those areas. Once you've completed your Strategy Profile, you can use the next tool to help you improve on it.

Strategy Stop Sign

One of the oldest types of American bridges is the covered bridge. It's estimated that nearly ten thousand covered bridges were built in the United States between 1805 and 1885. Once the car replaced the horse and buggy, however, covered bridges began to disappear. The ones preserved today add charm and character to their communities, but they generally allow only one lane of traffic in a single direction at a time. Consequently, stop signs are an easy way to help motorists know where and when to stop before crossing the bridge.

If only life were that easy.

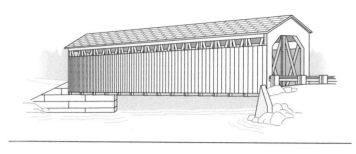

Covered bridge

Many people fall into the endless cycle of adding new projects at work and picking up new chores around the house until their plate is overflowing with stuff. We're good at adding things to our proverbial plates. But when is the last time you took something off your plate? When is the last time you consciously stopped doing something?

The Trade-off Matrix is a tool for helping us better understand what we should stop and start doing, where, and when. It offers a simple means of assessing the strategic trade-offs necessary to create a more effective strategy.

Following is an example of the Trade-off Matrix for the Strategy Profile created earlier:

Eliminate	*Increase*
Checking work e-mail at home	Time investment in community
Time-killing television	Financial investment in children's college fund
Decrease	*Create*
Total time at work by telecommuting	Monthly family outing
Attending meetings at work	Book club with friends
	Career support group at church

Figure 3.3: Trade-off Matrix

The work in this Trade-off Matrix helps the individual to better balance her investment of time, energy, and finances in areas that will give her greater fulfillment over the long run. When we record our strategy in the form of a diagram, as we did with the Strategy Profile, it makes a powerful visual statement. This creates a greater sense of urgency for making those important trade-offs. The Trade-off Matrix, then, is an effective means of altering your future strategy so that you make the most of your resources.

Focus to Succeed

Building effective strategies that stand the test of time demands commitment, discipline, and focus. Investment legend Warren Buffett is continually ranked as one of the top five wealthiest people in the world. When asked about the driving forces behind his unparalleled success, he responds time and again with one in particular: focus. Buffett discovered his purpose early on and has devoted his full attention to the work of value investing. Meanwhile, he has chosen not to invest significant amounts of his time in other areas such as travel, science, art, and literature. The discipline he has shown in pruning for extreme focus is built on explicit decisions of where and when to say "no." When asked about Wells Fargo's success in weathering the 2008–2009 financial crisis—the bank didn't allow employees to offer higher-risk mortgage loans—Buffett said, "The real insight you get about a banker is . . . what they don't do . . . And what Wells didn't do is what defines their greatness."[1]

While it may seem strange to think about what you're *not* going to do, there are plenty of examples to show the value of this approach. Starbucks has become a world-renowned brand, but CEO Howard Schultz acknowledges how easy it is to lose focus. He has said, "In terms of execution, we've unplugged a lot of things that were taking up mind space and time [e.g., hot breakfast sandwiches], and we've understood that less would be more . . . We were asking people to do too much, to chase after too many new ideas that took us away from our core business, so we pulled the plug on lots of things and focused on the ones that were most important."[2]

No doubt, you'll have business colleagues, friends, or family members advise you against focusing; they'll urge you to "hedge your bets" and "never put all your eggs in one basket." That's exactly what happened to Steve Ells, founder and CEO of Chipotle Mexican Grill. Since the company went public in 2006, the stock has risen 287 percent. Ells recounts the early "expert" advice he received: "When I started Chipotle, I didn't know the fast-food rules. People told us the food was too expensive and the menu was too limited."[3] Despite the cries from critics telling him not to focus, not to say "no," Ells has refused to expand Chipotle's menu beyond four options: burritos, burrito bowls, tacos, and salads. Says Ells, "We want to do just a few things better than everyone else."[4]

Apple has redefined several industries en route to its steamrolling success in recent years with the Mac computer, iPod, iTunes Store, iPhone, and iPad. CEO Steve Jobs has said, "People think focus means saying yes to the thing you've got to focus on. But that's not what it means at all. It means saying no to the hundred other good ideas that there are. I'm as proud of the products we have not done as the ones we have done."[5] He then gave a powerful example. For years, executives within Apple suggested doing a personal digital assistant (PDA). But Jobs's insight was that about 90 percent of people who used a PDA only took information out of it while on the road; they didn't put information into it. So he figured cell phones or smart-phones would soon perform a similar function, which would dramatically reduce the PDA market. Jobs said if Apple had gotten into the PDA market at that time, it wouldn't have had the resources to do the iPod. Apple's success is built just as much on what the company has chosen *not* to do.

The game of baseball can provide a snapshot of why it's important to focus resources in the right areas to be success-ful. During the 2001–2010 Major League Baseball seasons, the New York Yankees have won one World Series title. Win-ning even one title would seem impressive for most ball clubs. However, when you consider that the New York Yankees con-tinually have the highest payroll of any team, sometimes even two or three times the payroll, that single-win record exposes an ineffective use of resources. This shows that having the most resources guarantees nothing. It's how we use, or allocate, those resources that truly matters. Smith College economics professor Andrew Zimbalist offers this analysis: "The statistical relation-ship between a team's winning percentage and its payroll is not very high. When I plot payroll and win percentage on the same graph, the two variables don't always move together. Between 70 and 85 percent of a team's on-field success is explained by factors other than payroll."[6]

Continuum Estate is a small artisan winery in Napa Valley that has chosen to produce only one wine: an expensive red blend of cabernet sauvignon, cabernet franc, and petit verdot. The winery has consciously chosen not to offer customers a wide selection of varietals, potentially leaving millions of dollars on the table. The flip side, however, is that its competitors will not abandon their other varietals to produce just one wine— leaving Continuum Estate the leader in its specialized niche. Continuum Estate's visionary Tim Mondavi says, "The singularity of our focus allows us to delve more deeply into growing and making a better wine."[7]

Not-to-Do List

As the previous examples demonstrate, the key to an effective strategy is to find things to say "no" to, so you can take that time, energy, and money and focus it in more productive places. While most of us have to-do lists and the popular "honey-to-do" lists hanging on the refrigerator, the Not-to-Do List is far less common. The Not-to-Do List can help you achieve your goals by simply identifying areas and opportunities for improvement—things you're *no longer* going to invest time, talent, or money into. These *no*s create a new reservoir of energy, because you can now focus resources on fewer areas in order to be more effective at them.

Here's an example of a Not-to-Do List:

- Eating snacks after 8:00 p.m.
- Surfing TV channels when nothing good is on
- Criticizing others (family, coworkers, relatives)
- Impulse buying at the store

- Checking the BlackBerry during kids' games/activities
- Starting the day by checking e-mail
- Eating dinner out more than two nights a week
- Failing to actively listen to family members
- Spending the entire week's check without putting money into savings
- Adding to the gossip treadmill at work
- Missing morning exercise sessions

We need to be clear on our *no*s. If you're trying to live a healthier lifestyle, there are a number of things you can do. Understand, though, that the things you choose *not* to do are just as important. Exercising for one hour a day, five days a week is great. But if we don't say "no" to eating junk food every afternoon or stuffed pizza three nights a week, then all our hard work has been for nothing.

Working sixty hours a week, year in and year out, can help us earn the income necessary for a solid future—if we're investing part of that money in assets. If, however, we're spending money in an undisciplined, non-budgeted way, on things that aren't adding great value to our lives, we're potentially wasting those sixty-hour workweeks. When it comes to successful budgeting, the things you actively choose *not* to spend money on are just as important as where you are choosing to spend your money.

Track your spending and investing habits for one month. Any surprises? Do you see a disciplined approach to creating a sound financial future, or are you spending money as if you were a bumper car at the carnival, bouncing from one random purchase to the next? Are you investing money or spending it? Are your purchases primarily wants or needs? What are your *no*s?

We as human beings don't like to change. The Johns Hopkins School of Medicine reports several studies of people who underwent a type of heart surgery called CABG, or coronary artery bypass grafting. The doctors met with patients right after the heart surgery and told them they must make changes in their lifestyles, including diet, exercise, and medication. Two years later, the percentage of patients who did not make any changes was 90 percent. That's right—90 percent of patients made no changes despite being told that without those changes, they had a greater chance of dying.[8]

Keep this in mind as you battle the status quo of allocating your time, talent, and money to the same things in the same way year after year. A McKinsey & Company study of two hundred large companies showed that the number one driver of revenue growth in business is the *reallocation* of resources from underperforming initiatives to faster-growing ones.[9] Whether in your business or your personal strategy, you must be willing to change your thinking, your behavior, and your resource allocation—not once a year, but on a continual basis. Take a hard look at your business and personal strategies. How do they make you feel? Safe, comfortable, and bound to mediocrity? Or anxious, excited, and full of limitless potential? Do you like failing to live up to your potential? Do you like to get beat? No? Then do something about it.

RESOURCE INVENTORY

Create three columns, labeled "Time," "Talent," and "Finances." Under each column, list the areas where you're currently investing those resources. For example, under "Time," one might have the following: children, spouse/partner, work, friends, volunteering, church, exercising, television, hobbies.

STRATEGY PROFILE

To develop a Strategy Profile, complete the following steps:

1. On the horizontal axis, list the areas of potential investment.

2. On the vertical axis, rate on a scale of 1–10 your *current* (Today) level of investment (time, talent, or money) for each area, with 1 being a small investment and 10 being a large investment. Then rate your future (Ideal) level of investment (time, talent, or money) for each factor on a scale of 1–10, with 1 being a low investment and 10 being a high investment.

3. Plot the two lines—one connecting the Today points, and one connecting the Ideal points—on the Strategy Profile graph.

4. Identify the areas where there are significant gaps between the Today line and the Ideal line.

For each of the areas you listed, identify specific behaviors that need to be developed to reach the Ideal Strategy Profile curve; then create a set of action steps for reaching that goal.

TRADE-OFF MATRIX

Using the areas of potential investment identified in the Strategy Profile, determine which areas should receive no future resources (list these in the "Eliminate" quadrant). Then decide which areas should receive increased resources (list in the "Increase" quadrant) and which areas should receive fewer resources (list in the "Decrease" quadrant). Finally, determine which areas could be created that you have not included in the past (list in the "Create" quadrant).

NOT-TO-DO LIST

Create your Not-to-Do List by identifying the areas and activities in which you are no longer going to invest your resources (time, talent, and money).

CONSTRUCTION SUMMARY

Effective strategy is just as much about what you choose *not to do* as it is about what you choose to do. Be crystal clear on the things you're going to say "no" to when it comes to investing your time, talent and money.

A Resource Inventory begins the process of identifying what you have at your disposal in the form of time, talent, and money. Once you create this baseline, you can determine the levels to which you're investing your resources; this will reveal whether your resources allocation is helping or hurting your ability to achieve your goals.

The Strategy Profile is a valuable tool for visualizing your overall strategy. It sheds light on where and to what extent you are investing your time, talent, and money. Where you *think* you're spending your resources and where you're actually spending them can be dramatically different.

The Trade-off Matrix is a tool for helping you better understand what to stop doing, where, and when. It offers a simple means of assessing the strategic trade-offs necessary to create a more effective strategy. What do you need to eliminate, increase, decrease, and create in order to most effectively meet your goals?

We all have a to-do list. What most people don't have is the infinitely more valuable "not-to-do" list. Your Not-to-Do List can help you improve and achieve your goals by identifying areas, opportunities, or things in which you're no longer going to invest time, talent, or money. These *no*s create a new reservoir of energy, because now you can focus on fewer areas in order to be more effective at them.

Research shows that the number one driver of revenue growth in business is the reallocation of resources from under-performing initiatives to faster-growing ones. Doing the same things in the same ways you've always done them will yield the same results you've always had. Shake things up by reallocating your resources on a regular basis.

STEP 4: DESIGN

BUILDING YOUR BRIDGE

*To see what you haven't seen before,
with your mind's eye open,
exchanging the old for the new.*

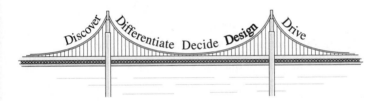

A useful feature in many of today's automobiles is the voice navigation system. Wouldn't it be nice if we had a navigation system for life—something to give us direction, help us make decisions, and keep us on course toward our goals? Imagine what it might sound like if the voice navigation system were applied to your life:

> **Voice:** Please enter a destination.
>
> **You:** I'd like to make a lot of money.
>
> **Voice:** Destination invalid. Please enter a specific destination.
>
> **You:** All right, I'd like to make $10 million.
>
> **Voice:** Calculating route . . . Expected time to destination: 127 years.
>
> **You:** What? No! There's got to be a faster way.
>
> **Voice:** Proceed one-half mile to the nearest convenience store and buy a lottery ticket.

Deciding precisely what we want, and designing a bridge to reach it, takes work. It's impossible to create a good plan without first taking time to strategically think about the situation. In the first three steps—Discover, Differentiate, and Decide—we reviewed a number of questions and tools to help you generate new ideas about your life strategies. Now we're going to explore ways to use those ideas to design and build your strategies.

When my cousin was attending college at Loyola University in Chicago, her father went to visit her apartment in the Lincoln Park neighborhood. After parking on the street in front of the building, he pressed the doorbell buzzer and was buzzed up. He climbed the two flights of stairs, knocked, and then walked into the apartment and sat down on the sofa. A minute later a woman wearing a towel, just out of the shower, walked into the living room and screamed. He was in the wrong apartment building.

Most of us have felt that frustrating—or in my uncle's case, terrifying—feeling of being lost. When we're traveling, we bring directions or a GPS device to prevent those moments, to help us navigate our way in an unfamiliar area. In the world of business, that device is often called a strategic plan. But in many cases, if a company's strategic plan could talk, it would say the following:

> Hi. Remember me? I'm your strategic plan. You don't call, you don't write—what am I supposed to think? Oh, sure, at the end of last year we were hot and heavy. We took that two-day getaway to the strategic planning off-site meeting, and you showered me with time and attention. You told me how much I meant to you and said we'd always be together. You even brought me to the annual kick-off meeting and proudly presented me to everyone. Then a few weeks passed, and I noticed you paying less attention to me and more attention to that slinky, young thing you call BlackBerry. After a few months, I didn't see or hear from you at all. I just sat on your shelf, dressed in this red, faux-leather three-ring binder, collecting dust. Now it's time to start planning for next year, and all of a sudden you're back, wanting more. Well, I'm sorry. I'm just not that type of plan!

Any resemblance between your business experience and the previous scene is completely unintentional . . . but highly likely. Let's face it: In business, many people simply don't use their strategic plan to drive daily activities. But if you're not using your plan to drive daily activities, you may as well not have one at all. In fact, that appears to be the case for our personal lives: As the research cited earlier, only 22 percent of executives have a plan for their lives. But what if you could design a plan that you would actually use to build a bridge to the life you really want?

The Power of Planning

Ever had your car break down? It's a deflating feeling. So imagine the angst in Michigan over the past decade as entire car companies were breaking down. After years of strategy decay, the US carmakers' inability to focus resources, make trade-offs, and create differentiated value finally caught up with them. But one American car company has emerged from the fog of failure to legitimately compete with the foreign players: Ford.

In 2006, Ford posted a $12.6 billion loss and was in a complete tailspin. It was at that time the company looked outside the auto industry, tapping Boeing executive Alan Mulally to try and turn things around. Critics were quick to deride the decision. How could someone with no auto industry experience possibly know how to lead a resurgence? Of course, the critics neglected to consider the fact that it was the leaders with decades of auto industry experience who had put the companies in these positions in the first place.

One of Mulally's first big decisions was to focus resources. He sold off Ford's PAG business, which included such high-profile brands as Jaguar, Aston Martin, Land Rover, and Volvo. He reduced the number of Ford chassis platforms from twenty to eight, and whittled down the number of brands from ninety-seven to closer to twenty, saying, "I mean, we had ninety-seven of these, for God's sake! How you gonna make 'em all cool? It was ridiculous!"[1]

During one of his first meetings with employees, Mulally was asked whether he thought Ford would survive. His answer: "I don't know. But we have a plan, and the plan says we are going to make it."[2] At the foundation of Mulally's plan was a mission simply titled "One Ford." It emphasized "One Team, One Plan, One Goal" and included the following four expected behaviors:

1. **F**oster functional and technical excellence.
2. **O**wn working together.
3. **R**ole model Ford values.
4. **D**eliver results.

Mulally distributed this mission on a two-sided card to all employees. He fleshed out this plan and has a business plan review meeting with all his direct reports every Thursday at 8:00 a.m. to discuss it. His approach was simple: "Communicate, communicate, communicate. Everyone has to know the plan, its status, and areas that need special attention. This is a huge enterprise, and the magic is, everybody knows the plan."[3]

In the first four years that he led Ford, Mulally's plan created a $19.2 billion swing, as Ford posted a $6.6 billion profit in 2010. The plan has given Ford direction, confidence, and the cash flow to invest in making better cars. The plan—and just as important, the new thinking that created the plan—has made a difference.

Do you have a plan? The research conducted for this book showed that only 15 percent of adults do. But wouldn't it be great to wake up each morning with a clear and concise guide to living a more fulfilling life? Imagine the hundreds of decisions each day that would be made simpler because of the strategic filter you developed in your plan, helping you decide what to do and what not to do.

A good plan begins with an honest assessment of where you are today. We'll review a set of three tools to help you leverage your internal capabilities (what you're good at) with your external possibilities (opportunities). These tools also give you a way to prioritize your resources for their best use and create strategies to do so.

BRIDGE IN PROGRESS

Well, I'll finally be retiring in the fall. I've had a good run— I'm finishing up a forty-three-year career, and I've had the privilege of being the CEO of a midsize manufacturing company for the past ten years. To be honest, the past five years have been tough, with the economy, the effect of low-cost labor in other countries, and trying to keep up with all the new technology. There have been nights when I couldn't sleep, worrying about how we'd meet payroll. I know a good number of the families of the folks who work at our company, and I couldn't help but feeling responsible for their well-being. But I'm leaving with the company in good financial shape, and I've begun thinking about what's next for me. I feel as if I've got some good years left to contribute, but I don't want to stay in the manufacturing field. I'm not a big golfer, and I don't want to sit around the house. I want to still be useful.

I've developed three- and five-year business plans for my company in the past, so I'm used to thinking ahead—just not when it comes to me. When you get up and drive to the same place every day, you're kind of on autopilot. Now that I'm retiring, it's as if somebody shut off my autopilot and I've got to fly the thing myself. Trouble is, the "thing" is *me*, and I'm not really sure where I'm headed. My next step is to try and design a "business" plan for me.

—Alan K.

SWOT Analysis

The SWOT Analysis is the most popular strategic planning model in the world. Developed in 1971, it provides a simple yet comprehensive method for examining the strategic fit between one's internal capabilities (strengths and weaknesses) and external possibilities (opportunities and threats). That is what the acronym SWOT stands for:

- Strengths
- Weaknesses
- Opportunities
- Threats

Strengths and weaknesses are internal factors we can potentially *control.* Opportunities and threats are external factors that we can only *influence.*

The SWOT Analysis model helps us answer two fundamental questions:

1. What do we have (strengths and weaknesses)?
2. What might we do (opportunities and threats)?

These four factors can be described as follows.

STRENGTHS

Strengths are those factors that make a person more effective than his or her peers. Strengths indicate superior performance or resources. Strengths are, in effect, resources or capabilities an individual holds that can be used to achieve his or her goals.

WEAKNESSES

Weaknesses are limitations or faults within an individual that will keep the individual from achieving his or her goals. These are points where the individual has inferior capabilities or resources as compared to his or her peers.

OPPORTUNITIES

Opportunities include any favorable situation in the environment, current or prospective—such as a trend, a change, or an overlooked need—that supports the demand for an individual's talents and permits the individual to enhance his or her position.

THREATS

A threat includes any unfavorable situation, trend, or impending change in the environment that is currently or potentially damaging or threatening to a person's ability to provide value. It may be a barrier, a constraint, or anything that might cause problems for or inflict damage, harm, or injury on the individual.

In general, strengths and weaknesses are internal and are made up of factors over which an individual has relative control. These factors may include the following:

- Resources (time, talent, money)
- Skill sets
- Knowledge
- Experience
- Relationships
- Values

Opportunities and threats belong to the external environment and are made up of those factors over which the person may have influence but has no control. These factors include the following:

- Overall demand for the individual's skills

- The activities of others

- Market saturation for the individual's skills

- Government policies

- Economic conditions

- Social, cultural, and ethical developments

- Technological developments

Following is a sample SWOT Analysis:

Strengths	Weaknesses
Coaching kids' teams	Not a good listener
Leader within Parent-Teacher Association	Too quick to judge others
Proven fund-raising abilities	Not fully engaged with family at home
Opportunities	**Threats**
Formation of church groups (2)	Third round of company layoffs (5 additional people by September)
Training for new managers (creating 3 new executive-led classes)	Community's lack of participation (attendance at events down 20%)
Suzy's interest in art (1 class)	Property tax increase (taxes now averaging 17.5% a year)

Figure 4.1: SWOT Analysis Example

Five SWOT Traps

As with any planning model, the reason a SWOT Analysis is performed is to generate insights about the individual that will help drive his or her planning efforts. To prevent your efforts from being an exercise in futility, you need to be aware of five SWOT traps:

1. **The laundry list.** When listing the individual elements under each category, careful thought should be given to the importance of each item. A laundry list of seven to ten factors for each category is fine in the first draft. However, only the three to five elements with significant impact on you should be recorded in the categories of the final analysis. Marshaling the mental discipline to create a tight SWOT Analysis enables you to move into planning mode with greater clarity and focus—two keys to a strong strategy.

2. **Generalities.** When listing the factors in the SWOT Analysis, there is a fine line between being brief and being meaningless. How many times have you seen a business SWOT analysis with "quality" listed under the strengths or weaknesses column? This is about as useful as putting down the word *the*. The same goes for listing "people person" as a strength in your individual SWOT Analysis. The factors listed need to be specific enough so that someone reading the analysis can understand to a reasonable degree specifically what is meant by the factor. Instead of "communication" as a weakness, record "unable to persuade others in a group setting"; this is much more helpful, because it alerts the reader to the specific cause of the communication issue.

3. **Special "effects."** Another common mistake is listing the effect rather than the *cause* of a strength or weakness. Take our example of "people person," which is often listed as an individual strength. It would be much more helpful to list the cause of being a good "people person"—for example, "active listener" or "high emotional intelligence." Listing a personal strength of "high net worth" is also an effect rather than a cause. What has driven your financial success? That's the cause you're looking for. Listing the cause plays another important role by allowing you to more easily identify and share best practices. Knowing what drives your strengths can potentially be applied to help other people.

4. **Mistaking influence for control.** Despite the clearly defined lines of strengths/weaknesses being internal and controllable whereas opportunities/threats are external and influenced, factors are often mistakenly placed in the model. The rule of thumb is this: If you can allocate your resources to a factor and potentially control it, the factor is a strength/weakness. If your resource allocation can influence but not necessarily control the factor, it is an opportunity/threat.

5. **Not quantifying opportunities and threats.** In physics, the mass of an object is a relative quantity. In the world of SWOT analyses, the size of opportunities and threats are relative quantities as well. If you list two threats to the financial stability of your family, yet you haven't taken the time to think through the numbers, then it's difficult to appropriately prepare for those threats. However, if

you list, say, one of the threats as reducing your income by $50,000 a year and the other as reducing it by $5,000 a year, then you have a better understanding of which threat you need to more fully prepare for. Sometimes we don't have all the necessary data to make an exact quantification of the opportunity or threat. That's when your expertise comes into play, so go ahead and ballpark it—give a rough percentage or ratio (e.g., property taxes increasing by 15 percent).

While it may not always make sense to put numbers on an individual's opportunities, thoughtfully considering how you would qualify those opportunities based on their value to your goals is an important step. If you have an opportunity to spend one night a week volunteering time to a nonprofit group or you can spend that time helping your kids with their homework, you need to first revisit your goals and decide which opportunity helps you meet them. Quantifying and qualifying opportunities and threats allows you to more confidently allocate your limited resources—time, talent, and money—to those areas that will provide the greatest return to your life.

Prioritizing Opportunities and Threats

Once you've identified the strengths, weaknesses, opportunities, and threats in the SWOT Analysis, the logical next step is to prioritize the opportunities and threats. An Opportunity Matrix is a valuable method of evaluating resource allocation for the opportunities you've identified. It enables an effective allocation of resources by prioritizing opportunities based on two criteria: probability of achievement and impact. Basically, you're asking yourself two questions for each opportunity:

1. What's the probability of successfully achieving the opportunity?

2. If you do achieve the opportunity, how impactful will it be?

Here is a sample Opportunity Matrix using the opportunities generated earlier, in the SWOT Analysis:

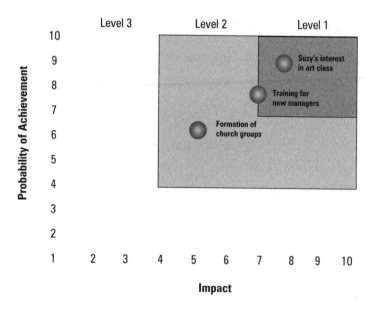

Figure 4.2: Opportunity Matrix

Once the model is completed, opportunities will fall into one of three levels, based on probability of achievement and impact. Opportunities in Level 1 should be given strong consideration for receiving a disproportionately high share of resources, while those in Levels 2 and 3 less so. As strategic thinking blends art and science, however, there may be opportunities in Level 3 that you believe deserve greater resources, even though the likelihood of success is lower. Those are the decisions you must come to grips with, and that is why numbers alone have never been enough to determine the most effective strategy.

The same exercise can also be run using threats—a Threat Matrix—with the only change being the label of the vertical axis, which should read "Probability of Occurrence" (as one is obviously not trying to "achieve" threats). Following is a Threat Matrix based on the threats generated earlier, during the SWOT Analysis:

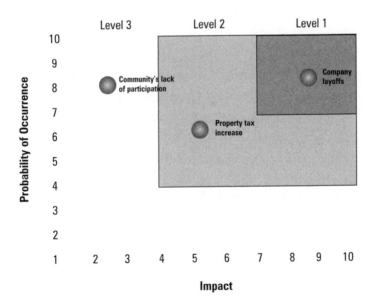

Figure 4.3: Threat Matrix

In this case, company layoffs pose the greatest threat based on the high probability of occurrence and the high impact on the person's life. Therefore, it would be important to develop strategies to maintain employment, whether within the current company or with other potential employers.

Creating Strategy from SWOT

The third and final step in our SWOT tool kit is the SWOT Alignment for Strategy. This model aligns the internal capabilities (strengths and weaknesses) with the external possibilities (opportunities and threats) to methodically develop potential strategies. It takes the essence of the SWOT Analysis and answers the question, "So what?" Based on the strengths, weaknesses, opportunities, and threats you've identified, what should you actually *do*? An example of the SWOT Alignment model (figure 4.4) is on the next page.

The SWOT Alignment serves as the appropriate final exercise after a SWOT Analysis and Opportunity and Threat matrices have been completed, because it leads you to potential strategies. Once these potential strategies have been created, you can channel them into a strategic action plan.

A Blueprint for Your Life

What do all the houses, buildings, and bridges in your community have in common? They all began with a blueprint. A blueprint is a plan. It's a detailed framework for going from dirt and clay to a finished structure. Bridge designers and architects like Roebling, Strauss, and Calatrava all used a blueprint to transform their creative visions into reality. We'll employ the

	Strengths	Weaknesses
Internal **External**	1. Coach kids' teams 2. Leader within Parent Teacher Assn. 3. Proven fund-raising abilities	1. Not a good listener 2. Too quick to judge others 3. Not fully engaged with family at home
Opportunities 1. Formation of two church groups 2. Training for new managers (3 new executive-led classes) 3. Suzy's interest in art	**Possible Strategies** 1. Use leadership ability to create proposal to teach new manager training class. 2. 3.	**Possible Strategies** 1. Increase engagement at home by taking art class with Suzy. 2. 3.
Threats 1. Company layoffs (5 people by Sept.) 2. Community's lack of participation 3. Property tax increase	**Possible Strategies** 1. Create fund-raising event for community to generate participation and raise funds for needy children. 2. 3.	**Possible Strategies** 1. Develop a survey and conduct it at local stores to gauge ways to increase involvement in community activities. 2. 3.

Figure 4.4: SWOT Alignment

same technique to transform your ideal life from a mere vision to reality, using a StrategyPrint.

A StrategyPrint is essentially a two-page individual blueprint. It serves as a real-time strategic action plan, guiding you day in and day out, helping you stay focused on the strategies that will drive your success. Having seen all too many strategic plans in the business world sitting in binders on shelves and gathering dust, I developed the StrategyPrint as a convenient tool to help people use their strategy to drive their daily activities. It can be used to capture the essence of a person's strategic direction. Visit www.strategyskills.com for a free download of the StrategyPrint template.

Page one of the StrategyPrint captures your Mission, Vision, and Values statements, and the current state and key insights of the Mind and Body. For each section, you should record goals, objectives, strategies, and tactics to give you an easy-to-use action plan. The majority of the insights and observations on your current state are developed on a continual basis through sound strategic thinking, using the questions and frameworks introduced throughout this book.

Page two of the StrategyPrint contains the current state and key insights of your Relationships and Finances. Again, for each section, your goals, objectives, strategies, and tactics are recorded to give you an easy-to-use action plan. The result is a common framework that can be used in your life to create, communicate, and execute your strategies. The StrategyPrint embodies the premise *less is more*. These days people are moving at warp speed and communicating instantaneously; the StrategyPrint enables you to think, plan, and act quickly and conveniently toward the achievement of your goals.

INDIVIDUAL STRATEGYPRINT®

	MISSION	VISION	VALUES
	Mission Statement	Vision Statement	Values List

MIND

State: Description of current state   **Insights:** Key learnings

Goals:	Goal 1	Goal 2	Goal 3
Objectives:	Objective 1	Objective 2	Objective 3
Strategies:	Strategy 1	Strategy 2	Strategy 3
Tactics:	Tactics for 1	Tactics for 2	Tactics for 3

BODY

State: Description of current state   **Insights:** Key learnings

Goals:	Goal 1	Goal 2	Goal 3
Objectives:	Objective 1	Objective 2	Objective 3
Strategies:	Strategy 1	Strategy 2	Strategy 3
Tactics:	Tactics for 1	Tactics for 2	Tactics for 3

INDIVIDUAL STRATEGYPRINT®

RELATIONSHIPS

State: Description of current state   **Insights:** Key learnings

Goals:	Goal 1	Goal 2	Goal 3
Objectives:	Objective 1	Objective 2	Objective 3
Strategies:	Strategy 1	Strategy 2	Strategy 3
Tactics:	Tactics for 1	Tactics for 2	Tactics for 3

FINANCES

State: Description of current state   **Insights:** Key learnings

Goals:	Goal 1	Goal 2	Goal 3
Objectives:	Objective 1	Objective 2	Objective 3
Strategies:	Strategy 1	Strategy 2	Strategy 3
Tactics:	Tactics for 1	Tactics for 2	Tactics for 3

Figure 4.5: StrategyPrint

The term *design* is normally used to describe the endeavors of those who work in the areas of architecture, engineering, and fashion. Rarely are the words *strategy* and *design* used in the same sentence, much less in the same concept. Yet, the definition of *design*—"the purposeful or inventive arrangement of parts"—describes exactly what a person does when building a bridge or creating a plan. To create the strategies we need to succeed, we must continually imagine new combinations of the main themes circulating through those four areas: Mind, Body, Relationships, and Finances. Adding to the degree of difficulty is the fact that these themes are constantly changing shapes and sizes. Life changes quickly, causing dramatic shifts in our situations and our resources. The StrategyPrint is a tool to help you make sense of these shifting construction materials, so you can design an effective blueprint for personal success.

Develop a SWOT Analysis for yourself by identifying your strengths, weaknesses, opportunities, and threats. After your initial run-through, consider soliciting the input of family members, friends, coworkers, and any others you feel might be able to provide valuable input.

To create an Opportunity Matrix, use the opportunities already identified in your SWOT Analysis. For each opportunity, determine the probability (on a scale of 1–10) of achieving the opportunity, with 1 being lowest and 10 being highest; also determine the impact on the individual (using the same 1–10 scale) if the opportunity is achieved. Based on this evaluation, place the opportunity at the appropriate point on the matrix. Repeat the process for each additional opportunity. Using the same methodology, construct a Threat Matrix by plotting your threats.

To construct the SWOT Alignment model, list the strengths, weaknesses, opportunities, and threats (identified in the SWOT Analysis) in their respective boxes. Then create potential strategies by methodically aligning the four elements:

1. Strengths and Opportunities (How do I use the things I'm good at to take advantage of favorable situations?)

2. Strengths and Threats (How do I use my strengths to reduce the likelihood and impact of these threats?)

3. Weaknesses and Opportunities (How do I overcome the weaknesses that prevent me from taking advantage of these opportunities?)

4. Weaknesses and Threats (How do I address the weaknesses that will make these threats a reality?)

Use the template given earlier (which you can also find at www. strategyskills.com) to design your StrategyPrint. Feel free to add, delete, or change any of the elements to make it as relevant as possible to you and your life. The most important aspect of the StrategyPrint is that you use it on a regular basis to stay focused on the goals you want to achieve and the strategies that will help you get there.

CONSTRUCTION SUMMARY

The act of planning creates confidence, momentum, and a more thoughtful approach to achieving the goals you've set. In building a solid plan, it's helpful to use a SWOT Analysis to identify your strengths and weaknesses and the opportunities and threats you're facing.

- **Strengths:** Factors that make a person more effective than his or her peers. Strengths indicate superior performance or resources. (These are what we're good at.)

- **Weaknesses:** Limitations or inferior resource investment that will keep a person from achieving his or her goals. Weaknesses indicate inferior capabilities or resources as compared to one's peers. (These are where we're lacking.)

- **Opportunities:** Any favorable current or prospective situation in the environment, such as a trend, a change, or an overlooked need, that supports the demand for an individual's talents and permits that individual to enhance his or her position. (These are what might help us.)

- **Threats:** Any unfavorable situation, trend, or impending change in the environment that is currently or potentially damaging to a person's ability to provide value. A threat is anything that might cause problems for or harm the individual. (These are what might hurt us.)

An Opportunity Matrix is an effective tool for allocating resources by prioritizing opportunities based on two criteria: probability of achievement and impact. A Threat Matrix is an effective tool for allocating resources by prioritizing threats based on two criteria: probability of occurrence and impact.

The SWOT Alignment for Strategy model aligns the internal capabilities (strengths and weaknesses) with the external possibilities (opportunities and threats) to help you methodically develop potential strategies.

A StrategyPrint is a two-page individual blueprint. It serves as a real-time strategic action plan, guiding you day in and day out so you can stay focused on the strategies that will drive your success.

STEP 5: DRIVE

CROSSING YOUR BRIDGE

You can feel it in your gut.
Time to make a move.
So move.

You know the saying *We'll cross that bridge when we come to it*? Well, we've come to it. You've surveyed, stylized, chosen, designed, and built your bridge. Now it's time to cross it.

What do you think of when you hear the word *drive*? Is it a warm summer day with the car windows down and a gentle breeze on your face? Is it a rubber-burning, high-octane race car, careening around curves and trading paint with other racers? Or is it something different, something ambitious inside you?

The word *drive* can be defined as "to cause to move by force or compulsion; to carry and guide the movement of; to keep going." There is nothing passive about it. Setting a strategy requires that you move from the passenger seat to the driver's seat. Recall the times you've ridden in a car's passenger seat to an unfamiliar destination. Did you remember exactly how to get there? No, because you weren't paying attention. Being the passenger doesn't require any of the effort the driver uses to follow directions, steer the car, make the proper turns, adjust for weather conditions, brake appropriately, and so on.

It requires energy and focus to drive. *Energy* is the capacity to do work. *Potential energy* can be represented by a book on a shelf. If the book falls off the shelf, that energy becomes *kinetic energy*. Driving your strategies on a daily basis takes kinetic energy, or work. That's why so many people are resigned to being passengers in life. They sit in the passenger's seat with potential energy that never gets converted into real work. Why? Because it takes thinking, energy, and effort to drive your strategy, and this doesn't fit neatly into our "instant gratification" society. It takes work to steer your life to meet the goals you've set. But just as when you're traveling in a car, if you're not driving, you don't have any control over where you'll eventually end up.

At this point you've discovered your purpose or mission (Step 1), you've identified your areas of positive differentiation (Step 2), made the decisions on where to allocate your resources (Step 3), and designed a plan to achieve your goals (Step 4). Step 5 in the process is to drive your strategies on a daily basis in order to reach your destination.

When lengths of steel, iron, or timber are framed together in the shape of a triangle to bridge a space, it's called a *truss*. Trusses can be found within the roofs of houses and beneath bridges to provide strength and prevent the structures from collapsing. Three elements comprise the truss for your bridge, enabling you to successfully drive over it to your goals: preparation, communication, and perseverance.

The Discipline to Prepare

When someone has reached a point of great success in his or her career or personal life, it's common to hear others say, "How lucky that person is to have been blessed with so much talent!" This is nonsense. Pioneering research by Florida State University professor K. Anders Ericsson has shown that when it comes to high performance, the cause is neither luck nor talent. It's deliberate practice, and lots of it. How much? About ten thousand hours of practice is required to achieve world-class levels.[1]

Don't confuse *experience* with *expertise,* however. Experience counts only when an individual is continually raising the performance bar and actively mining his or her experience for new learnings and insights. We've all been around people with ten or twenty years of experience in a particular area, only to realize they bring as little value to the job as a career politician does to—well, to just about anything.

Tom Brady is the highly celebrated quarterback of the New England Patriots football team. He has won three Super Bowls and two league trophies for Most Valuable Player, and he has the highest winning percentage of any quarterback in nearly fifty years. The ignorant would say, "How lucky he is to have been born Tom Brady!" The reality is, for the past two decades Brady has prepared more and worked harder than nearly everyone at the position. As a freshman in high school, he wasn't given a single snap as quarterback, despite the fact that the team didn't win one game that year.

When Brady entered the University of Michigan, he was listed at seventh on the depth chart at the quarterback position. Despite these hurdles, he worked himself into a starting quarterback role before he left Michigan for the National Football League. Once again, he was overlooked by most coaches and drafted behind 198 players in the sixth round. Bill Belichick, head coach of the New England Patriots, saw something in Brady, however, and later had this to say about the source of Brady's success: "He continually prepares at a very high level both on the opposing team's scheme and personnel. And he continues to try and have a better understanding of our offense, what options there are on certain plays and situations. He is always striving to get better."[2] Belichick also has said, "His preparation is exceptional."[3]

Brady himself credits preparation for his rise to success in arguably the most difficult position in the most dangerous pro sport. "The only thing I've learned is you really have to prepare," he says, "because when you get the opportunity, you never know what can happen . . . I don't want any unknowns. I don't want any guesswork. When I go out onto the field, I want to know exactly what we're going to do versus every defense we could face . . . I don't take the field if I'm not prepared."[4]

Preparation is about investing resources—time, talent, and money—in yourself. It's taking the time to think through the steps you've outlined in order to position yourself for the best chance of successfully reaching your goals. It's doing the research: talking to others and writing things down to help figure it out. By thinking and working through the five-step plan outlined in this book, you are preparing to reach your full potential. While *preparation* can often be an individual effort, effectively executing our strategies also requires that we *communicate*. We have to get out there and talk to other people.

Strategy Conversations

Just as a bridge allows the movement of people and products to their appropriate destinations, communication provides the bridge for moving strategic guidance throughout your life. If you don't have a strong communication bridge that connects all the key areas, information gaps can derail your efforts.

One would think we could easily learn how to communicate strategies in our individual lives by studying how it's done in the business world. Unfortunately, communicating strategy in business is not very common. A study conducted by researchers from Harvard Business School reveals that 95 percent of employees are not aware of or don't understand their organization's strategy;[5] presumably, then, business strategy is communicated only among the chosen few. This would be like the quarterback on a football team being the only player on the offense who knows what play the team is going to run.

The translation of goals and strategies to an individual's daily activities is critical to his or her achievement. From a personal perspective, it is essential to communicate your purpose, your goals, and your strategies for achieving those goals with the important people in your life. The people closest to you can be relied upon to provide input throughout the development of your strategies (Steps 1–4). They need to understand where they can support you and, in turn, how they can be supported in their efforts.

As you modify or change behaviors in your pursuit of newly created goals, consider how your behavior changes will affect those around you. If your new exercise routine is scheduled before the workday begins, what is the impact on the rest of the family? If you're intent on changing professions, what sacrifices will the family have to make? Openly communicating these types of behavioral changes, along with the mind-set changes you will be adopting, is a critical component of your long-term success.

A strategy conversation is a way of encouraging the exchange of ideas, beliefs, and opinions on the key elements of your strategy. The term *conversation* stems from the Latin *conversare*, which means "turning together." In a strategy conversation, the participants mentally move with one another from point to point, guided by five criteria. These five criteria include the following:

1. **Openness:** The ability to thrive in a situation in which the outcome is unknown

2. **Suspension:** The discipline to neither recommend nor criticize, but simply to take things in

3. **Candor:** The willingness to express exactly what you think

4. **Clarity:** The ability to concisely present your views

5. **Attention:** The ability to tune in and listen carefully to others

While certain criteria, such as *suspension* and *candor*, would seem to play against one another, using them at the proper moments can heighten their effectiveness. In my experience facilitating strategy development with companies ranging from start-ups to multibillion-dollar organizations, participants who embrace these criteria encourage the new and different perspectives that generate breakthrough strategy. Whether it is in one's professional or personal life, people with the know-how and confidence to mentally wade into conversations with uncertain gray zones even when they are not fully armed with every answer are the ones who fully tap into another person's best ideas.

A strategy conversation comprises two primary elements: *dialogue* and *discussion*. While the two terms are often used interchangeably, their differences shed light on the framework of a strategy conversation.

Dialogue is exploratory in nature. It involves the suspension of judgment in an effort to elicit the assumptions, thoughts, and beliefs of the other person. How often do we jump to a conclusion based on the first few words someone has said? We stop listening and begin formulating our response without truly hearing what is being communicated. And we miss potentially life-changing opportunities because we assume we know exactly what our spouse, partner, child, friend, or coworker is going to say. Instead, ask open-ended questions—a valuable tool in this phase of strategy conversation. Dialogue helps generate new insights when you allow yourself to be guided by a strong menu of highly relevant questions like those listed in this chapter's Bridgework Ahead.

The dialogue phase is used to unearth the key aspects of your individual strategies. Once you've exhausted the areas of strategic relevance with dialogue, move to discussion. *Discussion* consists of breaking down the insights or learnings generated through the exploratory phase of dialogue and using them to make decisions. Discussion moves you toward acting on the strategies—assuming accountability and deciding exactly how to implement them. It gives the strategy conversation its end result. This is where focus becomes clear, trade-offs are weighed, and decisions are made.

Unfortunately, many strategy conversations begin with a discussion mind-set. This inadvertently cuts off the innovative, assumption-challenging, and exploratory nature of dialogue, which is an essential element of an effective strategy conversation. And it results in the same, tired old ways that we've always approached things. Instead, detonate these broken-down bridges with rigorous preparation, open communication, and the will to persevere.

BRIDGE IN PROGRESS

I'm married and I have a beautiful daughter named Kayla, who is nine years old, and a feisty son named Jacob, who is five years old. About six months ago, I got a call from one of my two sisters saying that our other sister was just not making it, because of her problem with drugs. She has a fifteen-year-old son named Shane, whose father left when he was two, and Shane was basically fending for himself. My wife and I talked about it and prayed about it, and we decided to take Shane in.

Right away, Shane was a handful. He never studied his schoolwork, so we needed to sit down with him every night and go over his assignments. One Friday afternoon when he came home from school, I asked if he had any homework over the weekend. He pulled out a crinkled piece of paper dated three weeks ago for a book report presentation that was due Monday.

We sat down at the kitchen table and talked about what he needed to do: pick a topic, do some research, make an outline, type it up, and practice presenting it. He chose

Muhammad Ali, the boxer. He spent Friday night and all day Saturday doing research on the Internet. Sunday morning after church, he started writing, and by about three in the afternoon he was finished. He started putting on his gym shoes to go outside, but I stopped him and asked where he was going.

"Out to shoot hoops" was his answer.

"No" was mine. I told him he needed to practice presenting the book report. "Just like you practice jump shots and free throws," I explained, "you have to practice your presentation."

After dinner, Shane came out of his room. With me, my wife, Kayla, and Jacob sitting on the couch as his audience, he did his presentation. He surprised us all by throwing in some Ali impersonations. After a few more practice runs, he was ready.

Monday night, when I got home from work, Shane was sitting at the kitchen table with a big smile. He had scored a B+ on his presentation, which was his highest grade so far. Most important, he is starting to understand that you don't just practice for sports, you practice for school, too.
—Darren S.

Will Your Way Across

On December 1, 1951, a violent windstorm with gusts up to sixty-nine miles per hour hammered the Golden Gate Bridge. The center span undulated more than ten feet; it swayed sideways ten feet in both directions as well. Despite minor damage, the bridge stood. But eleven years earlier, the Tacoma Narrows Bridge in Washington hadn't been so fortunate. As the bridge was battered by forty-two-mile-per-hour winds, the deck's plate girders were caught up, leading to amplified oscillation and violent convolutions—and causing the bridge to plunge into the water below.

Tacoma Narrows Bridge, Tacoma, Washington

Then, on October 17, 1989, the 7.1 magnitude Loma Prieta earthquake struck the Bay area; its epicenter was located sixty miles to the south of the Golden Gate Bridge. While the nearby

San Francisco–Oakland Bay Bridge's upper deck fractured, the Golden Gate Bridge again stood firm.

Wind is potentially the greatest constant danger to a bridge, while earthquakes can wreak havoc on bridges within their vicinity. Solid construction and the ability to prepare for adverse conditions are keys to a bridge's longevity. When it comes to executing our strategies, we too must be prepared for resistance and seismic changes in our lives. In other words, we must be prepared to persevere when times get tough. As actor, author, and comedian Steve Martin has pointed out, "Perseverance is a great substitute for talent."[6]

Lady Gaga is famous for having a terrific voice, wearing that raw meat dress, and being a matchless entertainer. Yet the man who took her mainstream is not famous for any of these things. Nadir Khayat, known as RedOne, is a music writer and producer who has worked with Usher (on his single "More"), Mary J. Blige ("Whole Lotta Love"), and Enrique Iglesias ("I Like It"). In 2009, RedOne ranked first among producers and second among songwriters (behind Gaga); Billboard also ranked him in the top ten producers of 2010. He shared a Grammy with Lady Gaga for "Poker Face" and was nominated in 2010 for best album of the year (*The Fame*) and in 2011 for best producer of the year.

Behind RedOne's successful career, however, is a story of hardship. The youngest of nine children, he was homeless at age nineteen. "I did everything possible to survive," he says. "I would not go back home without making my dream come true. I washed dishes in restaurants. Nobody knew I was sleeping on the floor of a kitchen in a restaurant. I was crying a lot, but quitting was not an option."[7]

RedOne gradually made inroads as a producer in Sweden, and his "Bamboo" mash-up hit was chosen as the 2006 World Cup's (soccer) official melody. But this sudden acclaim didn't translate into sustained success. "I had to struggle more," he reveals. "My wife and I had an air mattress in our apartment—that's it. I lost all the money I had saved. There was no work. I never thought of giving up this dream until I got married, because here is another person to take care of."[8]

On New Year's Eve 2006, RedOne nearly gave up his dream for good. Instead, he borrowed money from his wife's sister and decided to hang in there for three more months. After continuing to persevere, several smaller pieces of work led to a connection with Lady Gaga. His perseverance had finally paid off. Now, singer and rapper Akon says this about RedOne: "From day one, I knew [he] was going to be one of the most prolific producers of our generation. I always felt like he had the right attitude and the talent."[9]

Not many people are willing to sleep on the floor of a restaurant in the pursuit of their goals. Maybe that's the problem. In a society where we can get forty-five variations of a cup of coffee and watch any one of three hundred TV shows at the push of a button, we've grown accustomed to getting what we want instantly. Why, then (the reasoning extends), shouldn't I be able to get what I want immediately at work and at home? Here's the answer: It's the same reason you don't get ripe fruits and vegetables the instant you plant seeds. It's the same reason a baby takes nine months to develop in the mother's womb. Growth takes time and effort. The goals you set and the strategies to achieve them are your path to growth.

In the research process for his book *Flow: The Psychology of Optimal Experience*, psychology professor Mihaly Csikszentmihalyi found perseverance to be a cornerstone characteristic of strong individuals. He wrote, "The ability to persevere despite obstacles and setbacks is the quality people most admire in others."[10] We cheer for underdogs because they're inherently at some type of disadvantage—size, strength, talent—yet they fight to achieve their goals. When the underdog US Olympic hockey team shocked the world by beating the formidable USSR squad before winning the 1980 Olympic Gold medal, it was a visceral reminder of the power of perseverance. The power of forging on when others around you criticize, doubt, or discourage you. The power of going forward when nothing around you supports that notion. The power of knowing you simply will not give up until you've reached your goals.

Harry Potter series author J. K. Rowling's first book was rejected by twelve publishers. Walt Disney was fired by a newspaper editor who told him he "lacked imagination." Michael Jordan was cut from his high school varsity basketball team. Business magnate Donald Trump has said, "I was relentless, even in the face of the total lack of encouragement, because much more often than you'd think, sheer persistence is the difference between success and failure."[11] If you are going to realize your goals, you will have to persevere. There are no pithy formulas for perseverance. It's simply a matter of refusing to give up until you've crossed your bridge.

Thirty-Thousand-Foot View of Life

When you have the supports in place to cross your bridge and follow your StrategyPrint, you need to get busy and take action. You need to execute your strategy.

Successful strategy execution depends on a system of interacting components: people, motivations, values, priorities, and so forth. Together, these parts make up the whole system. One of the biggest gaps I've seen in organizations is their not having a way to unite the system, to bridge the strategic plan with the smaller components—people's day-to-day activities. A Harris Interactive study of twenty-three thousand workers showed that 80 percent don't understand how their work relates to the organization's goals and strategies.[12] Think about where you work. Do you understand your organization's goals and the strategies for achieving them?

A way of bridging this gap between the strategic plan collecting dust on the shelf and the day-to-day activities is to see the big picture. We often hear strategy described as the "Big Picture," so why not draw that picture? You can create a picture of your personal strategic plan on a single page by using a tool called the Activity System Map. This map is an effective way to see and stay focused on your strategy. It provides a thirty-thousand-foot view of your individual strategy by capturing the strategic themes and tactics, and the relationships between them.

Designing an Activity System Map first requires the individual to step back and view the strategy from high ground to better understand the whole system. Then the map will help

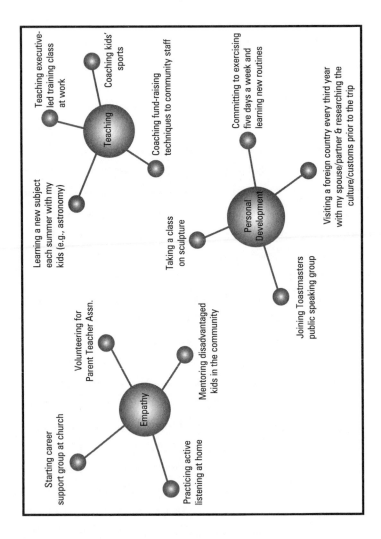

Figure 5.1: Activity System Map

you drill down into the system to assemble a conceptual framework, identifying the interrelationships and competencies of the key facets of your plan. Once completed, the Activity System Map will provide a clear and concise picture of your plan, which enables you to more effectively set direction and allocate resources on a continual basis.

The Activity System Map identifies the three to five strategic themes, the areas where the individual puts most of his or her resources to create differentiated value and to drive success, and the activities or tactics that support success. Figure 5.1 is an example of the Activity System Map for an individual. The steps to design a personal Activity System Map are found in Bridgework Ahead.

The Activity System Map simplifies the approach to strategy. It gives you a way to visually picture your strategic plan. It provides a powerful way to communicate the plan by helping you maintain focus on the important drivers in achieving your goals throughout the year.

The first key to successfully driving across your bridge is to prepare. First, review the Purpose Channeling exercise you completed for Step 1: Discover. List the steps you are taking to continually prepare yourself to reach the goals you've identified and the strategies for achieving them.

Communication is the second key to implementing your strategy. Inviting dialogue with key people in your life will help you gather input about your individual strategies. Use the following questions to frame your strategy-conversation dialogues:

1. How do you see my goals and strategies affecting our relationship?

2. Are there any aspects of my goals and strategies that are not clear?

3. What do you see as the biggest obstacles I face in reaching these goals?

4. Are there any other strategies I can use to hit these goals?

5. How can I help you use *your* strategies to achieve *your* goals?

6. How can these strategies be translated to other areas of your life?

7. Are there any barriers to successfully implementing these strategies?

8. How do your goals and strategies overlap or diverge from the ones I've outlined?

9. Have there been any recent changes at home or work that will affect these goals and strategies?

10. What creative ways can we use to communicate these strategies to others on a periodic basis?

After the open-ended, dialogue phase of strategy conversation has occurred, use the following questions to frame the discussion portion of the conversation:

1. Which strategies are you going to use to achieve your goals?

2. What are the trade-offs you're making with your resources?

3. Which goal is your top priority?

4. What new behaviors are you introducing in order to achieve your goals?

5. What old behaviors are you stopping in order to achieve your goals?

6. Which people are you choosing not to interact with?

7. What are you choosing not to offer to others?

8. How does your strategy differentiate you from others?

9. What resources are required to implement your strategies, and to what levels?

10. What are the main threats that might keep you from achieving your goals?

Use the following steps to design a personal Activity System Map:

1. Write down the three to five goals you're trying to achieve (see your input in the GOST Framework from Step 1).

2. Identify and plot three to five strategic themes (areas where you will focus the majority of your time, talent, and money).

3. Attach activities and/or tactics that are currently being employed.

4. Add activities and/or tactics that would strengthen your strategic themes.

5. Consider eliminating activities and/or tactics that have little impact on or will not support your new strategic themes.

After creating the Activity System Map, ask yourself these questions:

1. Do the strategic themes collectively embody the essence of my plan—a strategy that maximizes my differentiated value?

2. Is each activity or tactic supporting at least one strategic theme?

CONSTRUCTION SUMMARY

The word *drive* is defined as "to cause to move by force or compulsion; to carry and guide the movement of; to keep going." Once you've surveyed, stylized, chosen, designed, and built your bridge, you need to drive across it.

There are three elements that comprise the truss, or support, for your bridge, enabling you to successfully drive over it and reach your goals:

1. Preparation
2. Communication
3. Perseverance

Preparation is about investing resources—time, talent, and money—in yourself. When you take the time to think through the steps you've outlined, you can position yourself for the best chance of successfully reaching your goals.

Strategy conversations enable you to communicate your strategies to the other important people in your life. Effective strategy conversations include both dialogue and discussion.

Dialogue helps generate new insights. Open-ended questions are a valuable tool in this phase of a strategy conversation. Once you've exhausted the areas of strategic relevance with dialogue, move on to discussion.

Discussion consists of breaking down the insights or learnings generated through the exploratory phase of dialogue, and then using them to make decisions.

The Activity System Map is an effective way to see the big picture and stay focused on your strategy. It provides a thirty-thousand-foot view of your individual strategy by capturing the strategic themes and tactics, and the relationships between them.

When it comes to executing your strategies, you must be prepared for resistance and seismic changes in your life. In other words, you must be prepared to persevere when times get tough.

CLOSE

LIVING STRATEGICALLY

Spanning gaps, crossing barriers.
Passage from here to there.
It begins and ends with a bridge.

Sometimes it takes the unbridled enthusiasm of a child to remind us what's important. When my young son Luke sprang down the stairs that Saturday morning and asked, "Dad, are you ready for the greatest day of your life?" it awakened in me a renewed sense of purpose. By investing your time and thought in this book, you've moved closer to knowing exactly what the greatest day of *your* life would look like—and defining the strategies for getting there.

Think Time

As you continue to develop your individual strategies, the biggest obstacle you'll face is time. Time to think. Time to learn. Time to act. Consider your life today: How much of your time is truly at your discretion? At work, do you dictate how your time is spent, or is how you spend your time a reaction to what others want? At home, does time slip away into meaningless hours of television, video games, and Internet browsing? If you don't take charge of your time, you'll never take charge of your life.

In the workplace, research by Professor Heike Bruch of the University of St. Gallen (Switzerland) has shown that 90 percent of managers waste their time on all sorts of ineffective activities.[1] Professor Robert Kaplan of Harvard Business School revealed that this is true even at the highest levels of an organization, with 85 percent of executive leadership teams spending less than one hour per month discussing strategy and 50 percent of those teams spending no time at all.[2]

Contrast those examples with the approach of Amazon.com CEO Jeff Bezos, ranked by *Chief Executive Magazine* as the fifth most valuable CEO in the world in 2010 based on return to shareholders. Bezos has said, "We have a group called the S Team—*S* meaning 'senior'—that stays abreast of what the company is working on and delves into strategy issues. It meets for about four hours every Tuesday. . . . At different scale levels, it's happening everywhere in the company."[3] This shows a considerable investment of time spent on strategy. Clearly, it has paid off for Amazon.

Strategic people in nonprofit and for-profit organizations carve out blocks of time in their schedules for thinking. Joel Klein, former chancellor for the New York City public schools, understands the value of taking time to think strategically. Despite overseeing 1.1 million students and eighty thousand teachers, Klein didn't allow his schedule to be swallowed up by activity for activity's sake. He has said, "I learned when I was in the federal government that most people like to go to meetings all day, and I just don't. I try to block out chunks of time where I can read things more easily and think through the next moves and strategies. I'll have an hour of just think time. I make that part of my schedule."[4] How often do you schedule time to think about the strategic direction of your life? It's time to start.

As you set aside time to think on a regular basis, be prepared to consider what you've learned. A prime example of the importance of taking time to think and generate insights is Luis Alvarez, a Nobel Prize–winning physicist. A sample of his "thinking" accomplishments include the theory that asteroids hitting the Earth caused the extinction of dinosaurs, and the discovery of a large number of resonance states, made possible through his development of a technique using a hydrogen bubble chamber and data analysis. Dr. Alvarez credits his father for giving him the advice that shaped his illustrious career. Walter Alvarez, a renowned physician and prolific writer of medical textbooks, counseled young Luis to invest time each day to ponder what he had learned from his work. Luis took this advice to heart and spent a half hour each day thinking about his learnings and writing them down in a journal.[5] When is the last time you thought about what you've learned from your work or your personal life—and actually wrote it down?

If you don't find the discipline to schedule "think time," it simply won't happen. A study by Microsoft tracked the e-mail habits of employees and found that once their work had been interrupted by an e-mail notification, it took twenty-four minutes on average to return to the original activity.[6] Having the discipline to block out this think time actually translates into getting more done.

When will *your* think time be? Take a look at your calendar for the next two weeks and schedule thirty minutes of uninterrupted think time for each week. It might be during lunch, at 3:00 p.m. on Friday, or on the commute home with no radio playing. It might be when you first wake up or right before bed.

Then decide what you'll use to capture your thoughts. A journal, a Word document on your computer, or an audio recorder can all serve the purpose. The key is having the discipline to do it. Harvard researcher Leslie A. Perlow found that engineers who blocked out uninterrupted think time from the start of the workday until noon showed a 65 percent improvement in productivity.[7] While scheduling time "just to think" may make you feel guilty about "not working," the data shows you'll actually accomplish much more in the long run.

Drew Brees, the Super Bowl–winning quarterback for the New Orleans Saints and *Sports Illustrated*'s 2010 Sportsman of the Year, appreciates the importance of blocking out the seemingly urgent but unimportant. Brees has said, "You're always in a position where you have to eliminate distractions and negative influences in order to focus, concentrate, accomplish your goals. You just have to understand that your window of opportunity is a small one. You have to make sure you're doing everything you can within that window to accomplish what you set out to accomplish—that you've made that commitment to yourself, to the people around you."[8]

The Strategy Tune-up

Most people wouldn't think of going a year or two without maintenance on their car—changing the oil, checking the filters, rotating the tires. But many of those same people go twelve, eighteen, even twenty-four months or more without doing a brief tune-up or diagnostic check of their strategies. We arguably spend more time tuning up our $30,000 cars than we do our multimillion-dollar businesses or, more important, our lives. As you develop strategy for your life, it's important to give it a regular tune-up. Investing a few hours each month to review your goals, identify what's changing around you, and adjust your strategies accordingly will keep you on track.

Here's a checklist to use during your personal strategy tune-ups:

- Review the Individual Survey (Mind, Body, Relationships, and Finances) to see what about your situation has changed.

- Review the other strategy tools you used to create your strategy (SWOT Analysis, Strategy Profile, Activity System Map, etc.) and update them with any new insights or changes.

- Check off any goals that have been achieved, and replace them with new ones.

- Record the progress you're making toward your goals and objectives.

- If it doesn't appear you're making progress toward your goals and objectives, reconsider their validity.

- Consider modifying your strategies to more effectively reach the goals and objectives.

- Communicate with the other key players in your strategy system (spouse, partner, friends, relatives, kids, etc.) about your strategy tune-up adjustments.

Your Time Is Now

Is it time for you to build your bridge? Strategy is a bridge for getting from where you are today to where you want to go. Whether in business or in your personal life, strategy is how we plan to get from our current position to our desired goals. Creating a strategy for your life will give you direction, confidence, and the ability to shape your destiny. It is time for you to build your bridge.

As we move from one point in life to the next, we choose our destination and build our bridge. Without a strategy, or bridge, we have no clear way to get where we want to go. Without a strategy, we risk falling into gaps and being held back by obstacles. Without a strategy, we are powerless to create the life that we want. With a strategy, there are no limits to how far our bridge can take us. *Strategy for You* provides you with a five-step plan for creating the life you want—a plan designed to help you reach your potential and enjoy your life at work and at home.

Are you where you want to be in your career? Are you where you want to be in your life? You and you alone can set your strategic direction. You and you alone will decide if you've reached your full potential. You and you alone will look back on your life with great joy or great regret. The choice is yours, and yours alone. As you build strategies in your life, doubts will creep in. During those times of uncertainty, anxiety, and fear, remember these words:

MY BRIDGE

It cannot be done,
crossing from here to there.
Ground's too loose, water's too deep.
This bridge is for someone else to build.

If it were my bridge to build,
I'd have more experience,
be smarter, stronger,
more comfortable, less anxious.

I'd have someone to show me,
walk me through,
step by step,
answer all my questions.

But only I can build my bridge.
A welcoming sky whispers encouragement,
rolling waters peek upward.
Work on my bridge has begun.

NOTES

Introduction

1. Marcus Buckingham and Donald Clifton, *Now, Discover Your Strengths* (New York: Free Press, 2001).
2. Paul Carroll and Chunka Mui, "7 Ways to Fail Big," *Harvard Business Review*, September 2008.
3. Pablo Torre, "How (and Why) Athletes Go Broke," *Sports Illustrated*, March 23, 2009.
4. Mark Riddix, "Seven Costly Pro Athlete Screw-ups," *Yahoo! Sports*, March 10, 2010, http://sports.yahoo.com/top/news?slug=ys-investopediamoneyloss031010.

Step 1: Discover

1. Donald Sull, "Fast Fashion Lessons," *Business Strategy Review*, Summer 2008.
2. Stephen Covey, *The 8th Habit* (New York: Free Press, 2004).
3. William Joyce, Nitin Nohria, and Bruce Roberson, *What (Really) Works: The 4+2 Formula for Sustained Business Success* (New York: HarperCollins, 2003).
4. Matthew Olson, Derek van Bever, and Seth Verry, "When Growth Stalls," *Harvard Business Review*, March 2008.

Step 2: Differentiate

1. Alexander Tzonis, *Santiago Calatrava: The Complete Works—Expanded Edition* (New York: Rizzoli International Publications, 2007).
2. Ed Catmull, "How Pixar Fosters Collective Creativity," *Harvard Business Review*, September 2008.
3. Bernd Wirtz, Alexander Mathieu, and Oliver Schilke, "Strategy in High-Velocity Environments," *Long Range Planning* 40 (2007).
4. Michael Porter and Robert Hof, "How to Hit a Moving Target," *Businessweek*, August 21–28, 2006.
5. Phil Vettel, "I Visited Next Looking for Greatness, and I Found It," *Chicago Tribune*, April 25, 2011.

Step 3: Decide

1. Adam Lashinsky, "Riders on the Storm," *Fortune*, April 20, 2009.
2. Adi Ignatius, "We Had to Own the Mistakes," *Harvard Business Review*, July/August 2010.
3. Jessica Shambora, "Chipotle's Rise," *Fortune*, October 18, 2010.
4. Arianne Cohen, "Ode to a Burrito," *Fast Company*, April 2008.
5. Betsy Morris, "What Makes Apple Golden," *Fortune*, March 17, 2008.
6. Andrew Zimbalist, "The Yankees Didn't Buy the World Series," *Wall Street Journal*, November 16, 2009.
7. Bill Daley, "The Mondavi Legacy Continues," *Chicago Tribune*, October 13, 2010.
8. Alan Deutschman, *Change or Die* (New York: Regan, 2007).
9. Donald Sull, "How to Thrive in Turbulent Times," *Harvard Business Review*, February 2009.

Step 4: Design

1. Paul Hochman, "Ford's Big Reveal," *Fast Company*, April 2010.
2. Alex Taylor III, "Fixing Up Ford," *Fortune*, May 25, 2009.
3. Ibid.

Step 5: Drive

1. K. Anders Ericsson, Michael Prietula, and Edward Cokely, "The Making of an Expert," *Harvard Business Review*, July/August 2007.
2. Jim Corbett, "Brady Plows Through His Foes," *USA Today*, December 17, 2010.
3. Tom Pedulla, "Bold Brady Still Hungers for Super Success," *USA Today*, February 4, 2005.
4. Tom Pedulla, "Brady Still Has Something to Prove," *USA Today*, October 31, 2006.
5. Robert Kaplan and David Norton, "The Office of Strategy Management," *Harvard Business Review*, October 2005.
6. Steve Martin, *Born Standing Up: A Comic's Life* (New York: Scribner, 2007).
7. Edna Gundersen, "Music Producer RedOne Achieves Monster Fame," *USA Today*, January 25, 2011.
8. Ibid.
9. Ibid.
10. Mihaly Csikszentmihalyi, *Flow: The Psychology of Optimal Experience* (New York: Harper Perennial, 1990).
11. Donald Trump and Tony Schwarz, *Trump: The Art of the Deal* (New York: Ballantine Books, 2004).
12. Covey, *The 8ᵗʰ Habit.*

Close

1. Heike Bruch, "Beware the Busy Manager," *Harvard Business Review*, February 2002.
2. Robert Kaplan and David Norton, "The Office of Strategy Management," *Harvard Business Review*, October 2005.
3. Julia Kirby and Thomas Stewart, "The Institutional Yes," *Harvard Business Review*, October 2007.
4. Jia Lynn Yang, "He's at the Head of the Class," *Fortune*, February 19, 2007.
5. Robert Buderi, "Thinking About Thinking," *Technology Review*, February 2004.
6. Paul Hemp, "Death by Information Overload," *Harvard Business Review*, September 2009.
7. Alison Wellner, "The Time Trap," *Inc.* magazine, June 2004.
8. Mike Zimmerman, "Drew Brees: A Champion Never Rests," *Men's Health*, October 2010.

INDEX

ABOUT THE AUTHOR

Rich Horwath is a strategist, author, and speaker committed to helping people think strategically to live profitably. He is a former chief strategy officer, professor of management, and founder of the Strategic Thinking Institute. His strategy consulting, training, and speaking work with world-class organizations have been profiled in *Investor's Business Daily* and on NBC and FOX TV. Horwath's previous book, *Deep Dive: The Proven Method for Building Strategy*, has been described by the director of worldwide operations for McDonald's as "the most valuable book ever written on strategic thinking." He lives in Barrington Hills, Illinois, with his wife and two children. For more information, visit www.strategyskills.com.

Strategy for Business

"Strategic thinking is the most valued skill in leaders today."
— *The Wall Street Journal*

Research shows the number one cause of bankruptcy is bad strategy. If you can't think strategically today, you may not have a business or a job tomorrow. Rich Horwath can help your managers develop strategic thinking skills to grow profits, increase productivity, and create competitive advantage. Based on his book *Deep Dive: The Proven Method for Building Strategy*, Rich offers programs to help your managers develop a common understanding and tool kit for strategy.

Rich's proprietary Deep Dive Strategic Thinking Learning System can be delivered to your team in a half-day, full-day, or multi-day program, and includes assessments, group workshops, strategy templates, workbooks, and the Strategy Vault online resource center. Ranked the number one speaker on strategy by several national associations, Rich can also provide your group with a dynamic and content-rich keynote speech on how to effectively use strategy for business and personal success.

Help your managers reach their full potential by contacting Rich today at rich@strategyskills.com or visit www.strategyskills.com to sign up for the free monthly e-newsletter, *Strategic Thinker*.

Be strategic. . .or be gone.

". . . The most valuable book ever written on strategic thinking."

—James Floyd, director of worldwide operations, McDonald's

"Insightful and masterfully written with tools that can be used immediately. This is the best book on strategy I have ever read."

—Ranil Herath, president, DeVry Institute of Technology, Canada

Free Resources

Building a bridge to the life you want takes effort beyond reading this book. The following free resources are available to help you realize your true potential and create a happier, more fulfilling life.

QUIZ

So how strategic are you? Take the Strategy for You Quiz to find out.

TOOLS

Use the free tools to begin working through the exercises you learned in the book.

TEMPLATES

Build your personal StrategyPrint by downloading the free template.

DISCUSSION GUIDE

Lead dynamic and interactive discussions about the book in your workplace, in book clubs, at community events, with church groups, and at home using the free discussion guide.

Visit **www.strategyskills.com** to
access your free resources today!